A
GENTLEMAN
AT THE TABLE

OTHER GENTLEMANNERS™ BOOKS

A GENTLEMAN AT THE TABLE

A Concise, Contemporary
Guide to Table Manners

JOHN BRIDGES
AND
BRYAN CURTIS

RUTLEDGE HILL PRESS
Nashville, Tennessee
A Division of Thomas Nelson Publishers
Since 1798

www.thomasnelson.com

For Barbara Schneider,
who's never been confused by anything set before her
—J.B.

For Scott and Paige Sims,
who have inspired this book and me in many ways
—B.C.

Published by Rutledge Hill Press, a Division of Thomas
Nelson, Inc., P.O. Box 141000, Nashville, Tennessee 37214.

Library of Congress Cataloging-in-Publication Data

Bridges, John, 1950–
    A gentleman at the table : a concise, contemporary guide
to table manners / John Bridges and Bryan Curtis.
        p. cm.
    ISBN 1-4016-0176-6 (hardcover)
    1. Table etiquette. 2. Etiquette for men. I. Curtis, Bryan,
1960– II. Title.
    BJ2041.B75 2004
    395.5'4'081—dc22

                                    2004014390

Printed in the United States of America

04 05 06 07 08—5 4 3 2 1

CONTENTS

INTRODUCTION

At some point in every man's life he sits down at a table, and he feels alone. Staring up at him are the tines of forks, the hollows of spoons, and the blades of knives. It can be a terrifying moment, one that he has feared for much of his life.

Even his parents, try as they might, may not have prepared him for this moment. From time to time, his mother may have asked him, "What are you doing with that fork?" or "Excuse me, but whatever happened to your napkin?" His father may have asked him, "Would it have hurt you too much to stifle that noise before you shared it with the rest of us?" And for many gentlemen, sitting down at the table is still about questions such as "What do I do with all these forks and knives?" "What do I do when a lady stands up to leave the table?" and "What do I do when it is time to pay the bill or split the check?" Although dinnertime can be fraught with questions, this book is filled with answers.

A gentleman knows that, over the course of his life, he will sit down to many dinners that do not involve his mother. Whether it is a high-pressure luncheon during the job interview process, a dinner celebrating a good friend's birthday, or a first-time date on the night of the prom, he knows that now is the moment when he must go it alone. As this book explains, however, there is a logic behind the placement of every fork, every spoon, and every knife on the tablecloth. Even when there is no tablecloth, this book provides the guidelines a gentleman needs—whether he is attending a Fourth of July picnic or a Super Bowl party.

In fact, a well-prepared gentleman considers every meal an occasion—a chance to enjoy the company of others while sharing good food, good drink, good talk, and good times. He comes to the table happy to meet the challenge, to make conversation, and to dig into the casserole.

Then, at the end of the evening, once he has folded his napkin and put down his coffee cup, he will feel proud of himself and his own accomplishment. He may even wish that his father and mother were there to bask in the glow of the moment.

32 Things
Every Gentleman Should
Know Before He Comes
to the Table

A gentleman does not
"grade" the table manners of his
fellow diners.

———

A gentleman does not assume
that his fellow diners are "grading"
his own behavior.

———

A gentleman does not talk
with his mouth full.

———

A gentleman does not chew
with his mouth open, nor does he
smack his lips, no matter how
delicious his food may be.

———

A gentleman makes
as little noise as possible
while eating.

———

A gentleman does not
chomp on ice.

———

A gentleman does not
pick his teeth at the table.

———

A gentleman keeps his napkin in
his lap while he is eating. He does
not tuck it into his shirtfront.

———

A gentleman sits up straight,
especially at the table.

———

A gentleman keeps his
elbows off the table when
a meal is under way.

———

If a gentleman finds that he
has bread crumbs on his shirtfront,
he brushes them off.

———

A gentleman finds no need to
apologize for bread crumbs.

———

A gentleman does not
play with his food, kneading his
bread with his fingers or stirring the
last uneaten morsels of his dinner
about on his plate.

———

A gentleman does not
wear his ball cap or any other
headgear at the table.

———

If a gentleman is asked
to pass the salt or pepper, he
passes them both.

———

A gentleman does not
leave the table without asking
to be excused.

———

When a gentleman leaves the table,
he need not explain his reason for
asking to be excused.

———

A gentleman does not
lean back in his chair.

———

A gentleman tries his best not to
belch or burp at the table.

———

A gentleman knows that belches,
burps, and coughs can occur at any
time. He keeps his napkin ready to
muffle unfortunate sounds.

———

A gentleman need not use his
pocket-handkerchief to stifle a slight
sneeze, cough, or burp at the table.
Instead, he uses his napkin.

———

If a gentleman finds himself in a
situation, such as a fit of sneezing,
that necessitates the use of his
pocket-handkerchief, he
leaves the table.

———

A gentleman never
blows his nose at the table.

———

A gentleman says please and
thank you, especially to servers, in
a restaurant or in a private home.

———

A gentleman does not
wolf down his food.

———

A gentleman does not
slurp his soup.

———

A gentleman does not attempt
to cool his food by blowing on it.
If he fears singeing his taste buds,
he lets his food cool gradually and
undisturbed in its own bowl
or on its own plate.

———

A gentleman never argues
with a server, at a restaurant
or at a private party.

———

Whether he is an invited
guest or the host of a restaurant
party, a gentleman shows
up on time.

———

A gentleman does not
overstay his welcome. However, he
may linger at the table after dinner,
along with the other guests and his
host or hostess, knowing that such
moments are often the most pleasing
and satisfying of the evening.

———

A gentleman does not
loosen his belt, no matter
how discreetly, even after an
extravagantly large meal.

———

In any aspect of his life, but
especially at the dinner table, a
gentleman does not bite off
more than he can chew.

———

1

FROM COURSE TO COURSE

KNIVES AND FORKS,
AND HOW TO USE THEM

When he sits down at the table, a gentleman surveys the equipment set before him, just as a mechanic checks over the tools needed to repair an automobile or a doctor makes sure he is equipped with all the instruments to be used in surgery. Of course, using the wrong fork for the salad or reaching for the incorrect water glass is not as disastrous as selecting the wrong scalpel. But a gentleman realizes that not knowing his way around a dinner table can throw off the dynamics of a meal, leaving him on pins and needles and in constant fear of embarrassing himself. The good news is that with a little practice, a gentleman can maneuver his way around any table—be it at a Sunday luncheon at his grandmother's or a formal dinner at the White House.

If a gentleman discovers
that his napkin has slipped from his
lap to the floor, he retrieves it, if
he can do so gracefully.

————

If the retrieval of his napkin
threatens to disrupt the dinner table,
a gentleman simply turns to his host
or hostess and says, "I'm afraid
I've dropped my napkin.
May I have another?"

————

If a gentleman is served meat
in a private home and is not offered a
steak knife, he does not ask for one,
lest he embarrass his host or hostess
(who may not own steak knives or
who may assume he has found the
entrée too tough to cut
with a dinner knife).

————

Once a gentleman has finished stirring his cup of coffee, his cup of tea, or his glass of iced tea, he places his spoon on his saucer. A gentleman never places a damp or soiled utensil directly on the table or the tablecloth.

————

If a server offers freshly ground pepper for a gentleman's soup, salad, or entrée, the gentleman may accept the offer or decline it, no matter what his dinner companions choose to do.

————

A gentleman does not chop up his salad with his knife and fork before proceeding to eat it. If the salad is not served in easily eaten pieces, he cuts it into one bite-sized piece at a time, as he eats it.

————

At some elegant dinner parties,
a scoop of sorbet (usually citrus
flavored) will be served immediately
after the first course or after the
entrée. A gentleman does not assume
that his dessert has already arrived.
He recognizes this touch of cold
tartness as a "palate cleanser,"
intended to give his taste buds
a rest either before or after
a heavy entrée.

—

Unless he is confident in his
knowledge of china, porcelain, and
other ceramics, a gentleman refers
to the plates set in from of him as
"dishes." He knows it is always wiser
to err on the side of simplicity than
on pretentiousness.

——

Two Forks in the Road

When a gentleman sits down to a meal—breakfast, luncheon, or dinner—he usually finds that the necessary flatware has been provided. (A truly thoughtful host or hostess never puts out more than two forks or knives at the beginning of a dinner, as a greater number of utensils might be intimidating and confusing, and unnecessarily clutter the table.)

A gentleman will find the knives and spoons arranged on the right side of his plate and the forks on the left side. On all occasions, a gentleman assumes that he begins by using the utensils farthest from his plate. This means that, when he is presented with the first course, he uses the fork and knife farthest from his plate. Once that course has been completed, he leaves that course's utensils (fork, spoon, or knife and fork) on his plate. As each new course arrives, he simply uses the utensils that are closer and closer to his plate.

Only one general exception to this rule exists. When a gentleman sits down at the table, he may find a small fork placed on the right side of his plate, outside the knives and spoons. This tiny fork is called a shrimp fork or a cocktail fork, and is intended for use with a first course or an appetizer consisting of shrimp or other shellfish. Shrimp forks are seldom encountered these days. They remain, however, the only forks ever placed on the right side of the plate.

For the most part, when a gentleman sits down at a formal dinner, he may look at the table and clearly anticipate what lies ahead. If he sees two forks on the left side of his plate, he assumes that he will be offered at least two courses during his dinner. Any time his plate is changed or a new course is presented, a gentleman assumes that he is to move along to another fork, knife, or spoon.

Should a gentleman discover that he has run out of knives or forks before the last course has been served, he feels perfectly comfortable in quietly telling the server, "I could use another knife [or another fork]." He does not apologize.

If the utensils have been provided out of order and a gentleman uses them in the order in which they have been provided, the server is at fault, not the gentleman. A gentleman never corrects his host or hostess, nor does he correct a server employed by another person. Instead, especially at a private home, he follows the lead of his host or hostess. His role in the dinner, after all, is to be a gracious participant. He refrains from any behavior or comment that might make his dinner companions uncomfortable.

When Salad Is Served
as a First Course

A. Dinner Plate	F. Teaspoon
B. Salad Plate	G. Dessertspoon*
C. Salad Fork	H. Water Glass
D. Dinner Fork	I. Wine Goblet
E. Dinner Knife	J. Napkin

The dessert utensil can be a fork if appropriate.

When Salad Is Served
Along with the Entrée

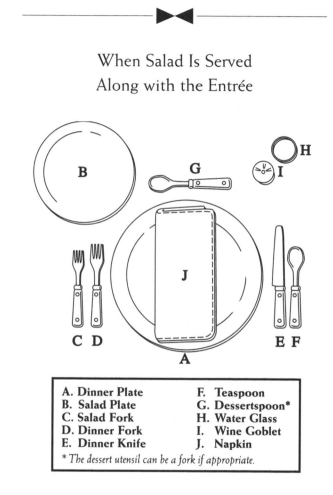

A. Dinner Plate	F. Teaspoon
B. Salad Plate	G. Dessertspoon*
C. Salad Fork	H. Water Glass
D. Dinner Fork	I. Wine Goblet
E. Dinner Knife	J. Napkin

The dessert utensil can be a fork if appropriate.

The Chair Man

When a gentleman finds himself seated next to a lady, at a formal dinner at a private home or in a public restaurant, or even at the most informal outdoor gathering, he always offers to assist her with her chair. Such graciousness will be particularly welcome if the lady is carrying her own plate or glass upon returning from a buffet line. If he finds himself seated between two ladies (as may be the case at a formal dinner party or even an informal one), a gentleman assists the lady seated to his right. If it appears that no gentleman is on hand to assist the lady to his left, he offers his assistance to her as well.

If it appears that the lady to his right intends to leave the table, for whatever reason, a gentleman at least makes the pretense of rising to help her with her chair. (In most cases, he will not actually need to stand up fully in order to be of help.) When she returns to the table, he assists her just as he did when the two of them arrived at the table.

Should a lady says, "Please, don't bother," when a gentleman offers to help her with her chair, he respects her wishes, although he still may lend a discreet helping hand if an awkward moment seems likely. In every case, however, a gentleman makes the offer, allowing the lady herself to decide whether to accept his proffered kindness.

THE NAPKIN

When a gentleman takes his seat at a formal dinner, or at a table in a restaurant, however informal, he immediately unfolds his napkin (even if it is made of paper), and places it in his lap. In this one case, he does not wait for his host or hostess to lead the way. If a gentleman must use his napkin during the dinner to blot his lips or wipe his cheek, he does so, always returning the napkin to his lap.

If a gentleman must leave the table for any reason during a dinner, he simply leaves his unfolded napkin on the seat of his chair. (A gentleman never leaves a used napkin on the dinner table until the final course has been served and he has finished his meal.) In some upscale restaurants, after he has correctly left his napkin on his chair, he will return to the table only to find that a server has refolded his soiled napkin and returned it to the table.

In such cases, no matter how fine the restaurant, the server—or the policy of the restaurant—is wrong. A gentleman never puts his used napkin on the table until he has finished his meal. Before he places his used napkin on the table, he waits, in fact, until the dinner party is obviously coming to a close, placing his unfolded napkin on the table as a declaration that he understands that the dessert has been served, no more coffee will be offered, and no more wine will be poured.

If a gentleman is the host of a dinner party, he places his used napkin on the table to signal the official end of the party. Guests may linger at the table as long as they like, but they may not expect any further food or drink to be served. The host may suggest, however, "Why don't we move along to the living room [or to the den] for coffee [or for an after-dinner drink]?" In such cases, the guests simply leave their napkins on the table and proceed to the other room.

A gentleman does not fret if he soils his napkin over the course of a dinner party. He understands that napkins were created to be used—not to be kept clean.

FINGER BOWLS

After he has finished his entrée, and especially if it was an entrée such as ribs or lamb chops that may have soiled the gentleman's fingers, a clear glass bowl of warm water may be set directly before him, on a saucer. Alternatively, the bowl may be set at the left side of his service plate. He will probably discover a sliver of lemon or a few rose petals floating in the water. The gentleman recognizes this bowl as his finger bowl, and he dips his fingers quickly into the water, brushing them with the lemon slice or the rose petals, if he chooses, then quickly dries his fingers with his table napkin.

After a particularly challenging side of ribs or a rack of lamb, a gentleman may be presented with a clean, steaming towel, with which he discreetly wipes his fingers, and even his mouth, before the next course arrives. After he has used this towel, a gentleman returns it to the plate on which it was presented.

When dining in a restaurant, such as a steak house, that specializes in entrées that may be eaten with the fingers, such as ribs or rack of lamb, a gentleman feels perfectly comfortable in asking the server for "a warm towel."

THE FORK AND KNIFE

At any breakfast, luncheon, or dinner a gentleman will be presented with two primary utensils: a fork and a knife. Depending upon the formality of the occasion and the number of courses being served, he may be offered more than one fork and more than one knife. He may also be presented with one or more spoons. But the business of dealing with the basic utensils does not vary—from course to course, from meal to meal, or from table to table.

A gentleman will always find his knife at the right side of his plate. If the knife is placed correctly, its blade will be facing toward the plate—a tradition based upon the assumption, for good or ill, that most gentlemen are right-handed. If a right-handed gentleman picks up his knife, with the blade turned toward the plate, he may plunge right into his dinner. A left-handed gentleman will no doubt have developed his own means of coping with the challenges of almost any occasion, culinary and otherwise.

In no case does a gentleman make a scene by examining the cleanliness of his utensils. If he discovers that one of his utensils is less than spotless, he simply asks for a replacement. He never attempts to polish it with his dinner napkin.

Dinner Knife

The dinner knife is the standard knife with which a gentleman will be greeted when he sits down at any table. Occasionally, he may also be faced with a fish knife (see facing page), which suggests that he will be served fish as a first course. If two dinner knives are set before him, and if a first course is served, a gentleman uses the first knife, farthest to his right, for his first course. If a gentleman has been served a course and he has run out of knives, he simply says to the server, "May I have another knife, please?"

Fish Knife

A gentleman recognizes a fish knife because of its wide, scallop-shaped blade, which is useful for cutting tender, flakey fish. If a gentleman sees a fish knife set beside his plate, he assumes he will be served fish as an appetizer or a main course.

Steak Knife

Steak knives are generally available in restaurants, and a gentleman may ask for one there. In a private home, however, a gentleman never asks for a steak knife. He fears that his host or hostess may not have steak knives readily at hand, and he also does not wish to offend his host or hostess by implying that the chop set before him is too tough to cut with a dinner knife.

Butter Knife

A gentleman finds his butter knife, also known as a "butter spreader," set on his butter plate, just above his forks, at the upper left-hand side of his plate. He uses this knife to spread butter or jam or jelly on his bread. It has no other function.

Dinner Fork

The dinner fork is the standard fork with which a gentleman will be presented when he sits down to dinner at any restaurant or any private dinner. If he is offered more than one dinner fork, he uses each of them as each new course is presented. However, if he sees a salad fork or a shrimp fork (see pages 27 and 28), he uses them in the manner described.

Salad Fork

Somewhat shorter than a dinner fork, the salad fork has wider tines, which make it easier for the fork to pick up slightly greasy, perfectly dressed greens. Although salads are sometimes served as a first course, a gentleman may also find them served after the entrée. A gentleman leaves the salad fork alone until the salad is served.

Shrimp Fork

Also known as a "seafood fork" or a "cocktail fork," a shrimp fork is only provided when a gentleman is served an appetizer of cold fish, shellfish, or mollusks. Unlike any other fork, the shrimp fork is set down at the right of the gentleman's plate.

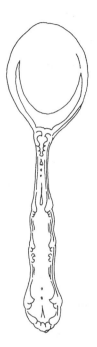

Soupspoon

A gentleman will find the all-purpose soupspoon at the right side of his plate. It informs him that he will be having soup as one of his courses.

This spoon may also be called a "dessertspoon." If it is intended to be used for dessert, the spoon sits above the gentleman's plate. He will recognize it because it will sit horizontally above his plate.

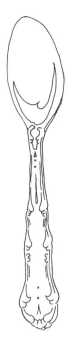

Teaspoon

If a gentleman sits down and finds a teaspoon set before him, close to his dinner plate, he does nothing with it, unless he is offered tea or coffee later in the evening. If he is offered tea or coffee, he uses the teaspoon to stir it gently. (He does not use his spoon to dip from the sugar bowl; he uses, instead, the spoon provided with the sugar.) In most cases, however, his coffee will be accompanied by its own small spoon, as will his tea.

Iced Tea Spoon

A gentleman uses the long-handled iced tea spoon to stir sugar and other sweeteners, lemon, and lime into iced tea, iced coffee, and other iced drinks. This spoon comes in handy because such drinks are usually served in tall glasses.

THE "BANK DINING ROOM SALAD FORK"

At luncheons in the dining rooms of some large gray-suit corporations, a curious dining-room tradition persists: The salad fork (the fork with shorter, broader-spaced tines) is placed inside, closer to the plate than the fork for the main course, even though salad may be served as a first course. Because a gentleman assumes that for his first course he will use the first fork available to him, this tradition has led to unnecessary discomfort for generations of uncomfortable job applicants. In such situations, a gentleman simply follows the lead of his host or hostess.

THE MULTITASKING GENTLEMAN

A gentleman may use his fork and knife in either the American or the Continental style. In the strictly American style (see page 34), he uses his knife and fork to slice a bite of meat or vegetables; he then places his knife on his plate and switches his fork to his right hand. In this style, a gentleman uses only his right hand to feed himself, making sure to keep the tines of his fork turned upward. (The process, albeit illogical because of the utensil switching involved, is not as elaborate as it sounds, and is the process most American men have been taught as children to use.)

The Continental style (see page 35) is much more convenient—and is the style many gentlemen find themselves using, no matter how they have been trained by their mothers. In the Continental style, a gentleman uses his fork with his left hand at all times, just as he found it on the left side of his plate. After using his knife and fork to slice a bit of meat or vegetables, he places his knife on his plate. He transfers his food from plate to mouth using his left hand, and with the tines of his fork turned downward.

A gentleman may use either the American or Continental style, anytime he wishes. He need not conform to the behavior of anyone else at the table—not even his host or hostess—in regard to this matter.

The American Style

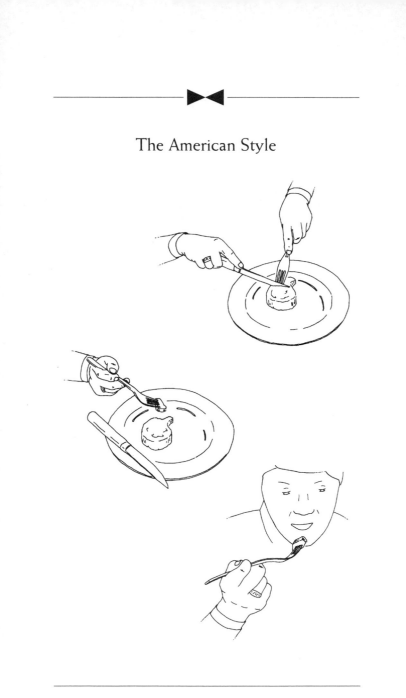

The Continental Style

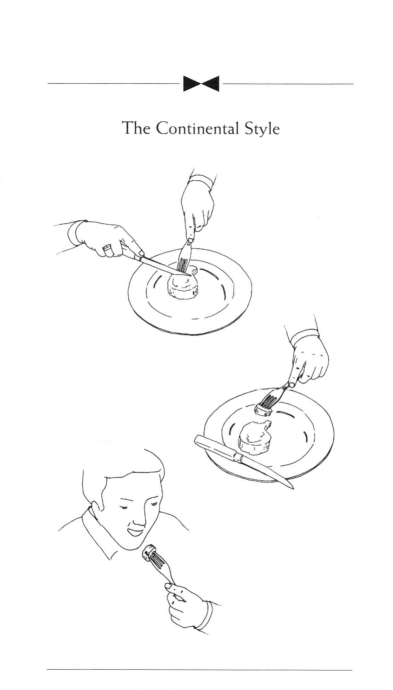

How to Use Chopsticks

At many restaurants offering Asian cuisine—particularly those featuring sushi, sashimi, and stir-fry—a gentleman may find himself presented with a pair of chopsticks as his only utensils.

The use of chopsticks is not a complicated maneuver. Here is a simple guide.

1. The gentleman places one chopstick in the crease of his thumb.
2. He braces the other chopstick against his ring finger.
3. He uses the two chopsticks, as if they were tweezers or pliers, to pick up bite-sized portions of food, dip them in soy sauce or other condiments, and then pop them into his mouth. (Sushi and sashimi are usually served in bite-sized or two-bite-sized portions.)

If a gentleman is not comfortable using chopsticks, he asks the server, "May I have a knife and fork?"

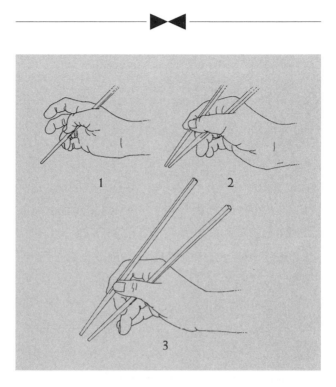

THE PLATES

When a gentleman sits down at a well-planned dinner, he will find that, along with the knives, forks, and spoons, a dinner-sized plate has been set at his place. This is his service plate. It is preset on the table so that the gentleman and the other dinner guests never sit down to a bare table, and it remains on the table until the entrée has been finished. It may, in fact, turn out to be the plate on which his entrée is served. In some cases, a gentleman will find that his dinner plate has been preset on an even larger plate, made of china, pottery, or polished metal. This large, almost shield-sized plate, is known as a "charger." Its function is largely decorative, but it also helps prevent dribbles of food from splashing onto the tablecloth.

The gentleman may discover that his napkin has already been placed directly on his service plate—in which case, he removes it immediately and places it directly in his lap. Or he may find that the salad course or appetizer has already been set out, on its own plate, atop the service plate. At an intimate dinner party (a table of eight or fewer people), he waits until all the other guests are seated, and until at least one lady has lifted her spoon or fork, before he begins eating.

If the dinner party consists only of gentlemen, he waits for his host or the guest of honor to begin eating before he plunges into his first course. If none of the gentlemen have been designated as a guest of honor—and in situations where there is not an actual "host" (as frequently happens at a restaurant)—a gentleman simply begins eating as soon as all the other guests have been served. At a large party or banquet, where more than eight people are involved, he may feel free to begin eating as soon as the guests on either side of him have been served. He knows that if he waits until a dozen people, much less two hundred people, have been served, his soup will grow cold or his salad will grow limp.

On some occasions, such as luncheons or casual dinners, a gentleman may discover that his salad plate has been placed just above his forks, at the upper left side of his service plate. In such cases, he assumes that he will be expected to eat his salad as an accompaniment to his main course.

GLASSWARE

Across the course of time, cups and glasses have been specifically designed or developed for virtually every possible beverage. A gentleman learns to recognize them so that when he sits down at the table, he already knows what he will be offered to drink during the evening.

Water Glass

The water glass is large enough so that it will not need to be refilled with great frequency. It may also be used for iced tea or soda.

White Wine

A white wine glass has a long stem and a slender globe. The shape has evolved to keep the drinker's fingers away from the glass so that the wine stays as cool as possible. The tall glass does its best to prevent the tart liveliness of the white wine from evaporating.

Red Wine

The red wine glass serves precisely the opposite function from that of its white wine brother. The globe of the red wine glass is wide shaped so that it may be coddled in the hand, allowing the wine to be subtly warmed by the touch of a palm.

Champagne Flute

The elegant champagne flute
helps preserve the bubbles of
the exquisite, celebratory wine
for which it is intended. Its
delicate shape helps contain the
champagne's effervescence.

Highball

The tall, cylindrical highball
glass is useful at any bar or
party. It can be used for iced
tea, soda, or any combination
of liquor and a "mixer" (which
means tonic water, soda
water, cranberry juice, orange
juice, or any other non-
alcoholic beverage). The mix of a liquor and a
"mixer" is what makes a drink a "highball." If
the drink consists entirely of liquors, as with a
martini, then, and only then, it is called a
"cocktail."

Old-fashioned

The squat, thick-glassed old-fashioned is the preferred glass for drinks of undiluted liquors, such as Scotch on the rocks, or a martini on the rocks. ("On the rocks" means simply that the liquor, or mix of liquors, is served over ice, as opposed to being served "up," without ice.) The old-fashioned takes its name from one of the great cocktails of the 1920s and '30s, a mixture of bourbon, bitters, orange, and sugar, muddled together with a splash of soda and served in a short glass.

Double Old-fashioned

The taller, double old-fashioned has become the classic cocktail glass. It may be used for iced tea, for a soda, for vodka mixed with tonic, or for any other simple cocktail. It provides more room for liquid, or liquor and mixer, than a simple old-fashioned allows.

Brandy Snifter

The snifter was created to be cradled in the palm, since brandy—which warms the soul and body—glows even more warmly when held in the gentle grasp of a caressing hand. Its balloon-like shape allows the aromatics of a brandy or liqueur to aerate, but it also concentrates the delicious perfumes through its narrowed "mouth." A snifter of fine brandy is the perfect, comforting close to a lovely dinner, but a gentleman takes care when treating himself to more than one.

Liqueur Glass

Set on a slender stem, the small liqueur glass (also known as a "cordial glass") is used for after-dinner drinks such as crème de menthe, Bénédictine, or amaretto. Especially if the glass is more bowl shaped, it may also be used for an after-dinner wine, such as port.

Demitasse

A gentleman may be presented with a demitasse— a straight-sided, miniature coffee cup containing extremely strong (perhaps flavored) coffee—at the end of his dinner, most likely when dessert is served, or when chocolates are passed in the lingering time after the actual dinner is done. He may either accept or decline a demitasse. He may request decaf if he chooses, but a decaf demitasse obviates the shock of caffeine, which is the reason this tiny coffee cup was invented.

Finishing Up

When a gentleman has finished any course of his meal, he leaves his used knife, fork, or spoon on the plate, or in the bowl from which he has just eaten. He never places a used utensil directly on the dinner table. When a gentleman has finished his entrée, it is traditional to place his knife and fork, side by side, on his plate, to indicate that he has finished eating. He places his used utensils on the lower right-hand side of his plate, pointing toward the center of the plate as shown in the illustration.

A gentleman may then expect a server, or his host or hostess, to take away the dinner plate, removing it from the right side of the gentleman's place at the table.

If salad has not been served earlier during the meal, a gentleman may expect that it will be served now.

At some particularly gracious dinner parties, a platter of cheeses, perhaps accompanied by fruit and bread or crackers, may be offered after the salad course but before dessert. Port may be served to accompany the cheese course. After a heavy meal involving a cheese plate, a gentleman does not expect a flamboyant dessert. Instead, he expects to be served a selection of chocolates or small cakes and tarts, accompanied by coffee, brandy, or liqueurs. At this point in the evening, if a gentleman feels he has already been plentifully served, he may simply say, "Thanks, but I believe I'll just have another glass of water."

If there is no cheese course, dessert follows directly after the entrée. In such cases, it may be accompanied by a dessert wine, champagne, or coffee. When a gentleman first sits down at the table, he may find that a spoon, a fork, or a spoon and fork, have been set directly above his plate. If no dessertspoon or fork has been preset, he is confident that it will be provided whenever the dessert is served.

It is traditional for servers to remove each diner's plate as soon as it is empty, or as soon as that diner indicates that he or she has finished with that particular course. This practice means that the diners are not left with their dirty plates staring up at them. (A gentleman indicates that he has finished by placing his knife and fork side by side on his plate, as explained previously. Alternatively, the server may ask him, "Are you finished, sir?" to which he responds, "Yes, thank you," or "I think I'll finish the last couple of bites.")

Nowadays, however, a gentleman may ask that his plate not be cleared away until all his fellow diners are finished. His intention, of course, is that no lonely diner will be left to finish his or her meal while the rest of the diners stare down at the empty tablecloth. When dining with four or fewer people, a gentleman may do as he pleases at this moment in the dinner. When he is a guest at a larger party, he is well advised to follow the example set by his host or hostess.

PLACE CARDS AND MENU CARDS

When a gentleman arrives at a dinner party, he may discover that place cards have been set out on the table. He understands that his host or hostess will have given some thought to the arrangement of the guests. He also understands that his host or hostess will have consciously decided not to seat him next to his spouse or his date for the evening, as it is assumed that there will be other times when the gentleman can enjoy that person's company.

A gentleman feels free to check out the seating arrangement, even before the entire party is called to the table. If he discovers that he has been seated next to a person whose company he does not enjoy (perhaps even a guest with whom he has had a recent argument), he may ask his host or hostess if his place card may be moved. (He does not take it upon himself to rearrange the carefully planned table.) The host or hostess may agree to make the switch, or it may turn out that the change of place may require a reseating of the entire table—a complexity the host or hostess has no time to deal with at the last minute. If that turns out to be the case, a gentleman simply bucks up and makes the best of the evening, knowing that the dinner will be over within an hour or two.

Once he is seated at his table, a gentleman may find a menu card, outlining the courses for the dinner or luncheon, in front of his plate or between him and his closest dining companion. A gentleman feels free to pick up the menu card and examine it, but he always puts it back on the table where he found it, so that it serves its purpose for others at the table.

2

A Gentleman
Faces His Food

Skillful Maneuvers at the Table

A gentleman understands that eating is a craft, a craft that sometimes requires finely honed skills, special tools, and unflagging attention to the job at hand. A gentleman should never feel threatened by any dish that is put before him, but he will be wise to acquaint himself with the tabletop challenges discussed in this chapter. He may encounter some of them, like a plate of escargot, only on the rarest of occasions, but he may be treated to a bowl of fettuccine at any moment, and on any day or evening he may be faced with a wedge of lemon. Squeezing a lemon wedge, he thinks, is a simple enough task, but he surely can remember times when he has sent a spray of lemon juice sailing into a nearby diner's eye. To avoid even this sort of annoyance requires forethought and a bit of acquired skill.

A gentleman never
calls attention to another person's
poor table manners, unless that
person is his own child.

———

Unless he foresees a disaster,
such as an overturned soda or a
spilled bowl of soup, a gentleman
does not correct the manners of even
his own child while in the presence
of non–family members.

———

If a gentleman is dining
in a restaurant and has not been
provided with the proper utensil for
the food set before him, he asks his
server for it immediately.

———

If a gentleman is hosting
an event in his home, he provides the
proper utensils for the dishes he is
serving. If a gentleman does not have
the proper utensils, he adjusts his
menu accordingly.

———

The Breaking of Bread

A gentleman may expect to find bread—it may be a hard roll, a soft roll, a slice of sourdough, or bread of any type—offered to him at any luncheon or dinner gathering. At a restaurant or at a private club where he is a guest (at a large wedding reception or rehearsal dinner, for example), he simply tells the server, "We'd like some bread here, if you please." When the breadbasket arrives, he says, "Thank you." If he sees that bread is not being served at other tables in the room, he does not ask for it.

At many restaurants, banquet halls, or private dinners, a gentleman will be furnished a bread plate. He will find this bread plate—a small plate, perhaps with a small knife set across it— set above the forks, at the upper left hand of his luncheon or dinner plate. The knife set across his bread plate is his butter knife. He uses it to spread butter on his bread. A butter knife serves no other purpose during the course of any meal.

If a breadbasket is passed from person to person, at any dinner or luncheon, public or private, a gentleman takes a roll or a slice of bread from the basket. If the bread slices are slender or the rolls are small, and if the gentleman is particularly hungry, he may take more than one slice of bread or more than one roll. He does not, however, help himself to more than one piece if by so doing he would empty the breadbasket. Neither does he "stockpile" rolls or slices of bread, as if he will never eat again.

At a dinner table, when a gentleman discovers that the breadbasket has been placed directly in front of him or within his easy reach, he does not hesitate. If he chooses to do so, he takes a roll or a slice of bread from the basket, places it on his bread plate, and then passes the basket along. If a plate of butter pats, or butter in any form, is provided, he takes what he pleases and passes it along as well. A gentleman passes bread and butter, or any other dish, around the table clockwise, which means that he passes it to his left.

At many fine restaurants, society dinners, and swell private parties, bread may be served, but a gentleman may discover that no bread plate has been provided. He may come to the table, only to find that a large roll has been placed directly on the table, at the left side of his plate, just above the forks. In most situations, this will be the only bread he will be offered throughout the first course and the entrée. Once a gentleman has begun eating this roll, he places it on his plate. A gentleman never places even a bit of gravied or buttered bread on the tablecloth. He does his best not to soil the table linen.

When a gentleman is served bread, he actually "breaks" it before consuming it. Whether he has taken a roll or a slice of bread, a gentleman always breaks his bread into a bite-sized portion, one piece at a time, as he eats it. Doing otherwise, of course, might allow bits of bread to go dry upon his plate. He butters each morsel of bread, or dips it into the olive oil, seconds before he intends to pop it in his mouth. Even with a freshly baked roll, a gentleman resists the temptation to slather the entire thing with butter, as he might inadvertently find his fingers covered with grease after every bite of bread. In the privacy of his own home, a gentleman may indulge himself in such pleasures, but he does not allow himself these private indulgences in front of others.

In the Soup

In many households and at many formal dinners, soup is offered as the first course. The soup bowl or cup will be placed directly in front of the gentleman, on top of his service plate. Crackers or toasted bread may be offered along with the soup, and he takes them if he wishes to do so.

If there are women at the table, a gentleman waits until his hostess or some other lady has lifted her spoon before he picks up his soupspoon and begins to eat. (His soupspoon will be the large wide-bowled spoon farthest to his right.) If there are no women at the table, in this matter as in all others, he follows the lead of his host, or he waits for the guest of honor to lead the way. If there is no clearly designated "guest of honor," he waits until his dinner companions have been served and then proceeds to enjoy his soup.

When scooping up his soup, a gentleman always uses the spoon to scoop away from himself, thereby reducing the likelihood of dribbles. If he wants to enjoy the final spoonfuls of soup, a gentleman tips the soup bowl up and away from him, to make it easier to scoop the soup up onto his spoon. Once he has finished his soup or consumed as much of it as he desires, he returns his spoon to his bowl.

Should a gentleman be served a soup, such as shrimp bisque, that he cannot eat because of an allergy, dietary restrictions, or any other reason, he has two options. He may simply place his spoon in his soup dish and enjoy a few crackers or a bit of toast. Or he may decline to take any soup at all. If he is asked, "Is there something wrong with your soup?" he simply replies, "It looks beautiful. I just don't eat shrimp."

The Terror of the Tea Bag

When a gentleman orders a cup of tea in a restaurant, he will most likely be provided with an empty cup (usually with its own saucer), a tea bag, and a small pot of hot water. In short, he will be provided with the equipment necessary for him to brew his own tea.

He proceeds to place the tea bag in his cup and pours the hot water over it. After he has allowed the tea to steep for three to five minutes (the longer it steeps, of course, the stronger it will be), he removes the tea bag from his cup and places it on his saucer. If no saucer is provided, he places the used tea bag on the rim of his bread plate. If no bread plate is provided, he has no option except to place the tea bag on the rim of his dinner or dessert plate. In no case does he squeeze the bag against the rim of his teacup, as if he were attempting to extrude the last dribble of flavor. If a gentleman wishes to add lemon and sugar to his tea, he adds them after he has removed his tea bag from the cup.

28 Challenging Foods and How to Eat Them

Be it a wedge of cantaloupe served in its rind at a restaurant, or corn on the cob and fried chicken served at a picnic, a gentleman never knows when he will come up against a dining challenge. While the temptation when eating alone is to do whatever is easiest, a gentleman knows that when dining in the presence of others there are rules to be followed. A gentleman never finds it tedious to follow such rules because he knows that they exist to make his life easier and maybe even a good deal less messy. This list offers guidelines for some tried and true techniques of the table.

Artichokes: If a gentleman is served an artichoke, it will usually be served to him whole, its leaves pointing upward. A gentleman pulls each leaf off, dips it in the sauce (if a sauce has been provided), and scrapes it between his teeth to remove the tender flesh. Once all the leaves are gone, a hairy little island will remain in the middle of the artichoke. This is the "choke." A gentleman uses his knife and fork to slice it away, uncovering the delicious artichoke "heart" underneath. He cuts the heart into bite-sized pieces and dips them in the sauce before eating them. A finger bowl may be placed on the table so that he may clean his fingers.

Asparagus: If asparagus is served cold, without any sauce, a gentleman may eat it with his fingers. If he prefers, he may use his knife and fork, of course.

Avocado: A gentleman may sometimes encounter an avocado, unpeeled but cut in half, and topped with some filling, such as chicken or seafood salad. In such cases, if the avocado is sufficiently ripe, he uses his spoon to scoop out the tender, creamy green flesh. If the avocado is underripe, however, he does not attempt to eat it at all, since both its texture and its taste are sure to be unappetizing. If a gentleman encounters cubes of peeled avocado, as part of a salad, he eats them with his fork.

Bacon: If bacon is crisply cooked, a gentleman may eat it with his fingers. If the bacon is still a bit limp and greasy, he uses his knife and fork.

Caviar: Caviar is most often served as an hors d'oeuvre, heaped on crackers or toast, or spooned into scooped-out new potatoes. It may, however, also be served as a first course, presented in a small dish set in a small bowl of ice, with crusts of bread and a variety of traditional accompaniments, such as grated onion, sieved egg, and capers. A gentleman remembers that caviar is salty and that a little goes a long way. He uses his napkin carefully because black fish eggs can make an ugly stain on the front of his dress shirt.

Cherry tomatoes: A cherry tomato may prove to be sweet and juicy, any time of the year, but its juiciness can lead to problems. Whether he encounters one in his salad or on his dinner plate, a gentleman spears the cherry tomato with his fork. If it is bite-sized he pops the whole thing into his mouth. If it is too large to consume in one bite, a gentleman uses his knife and fork to cut it in half. He never simply bites into a cherry tomato, for fear of squirting his fellow diners with juice and seeds.

Corn on the cob: Corn on the cob is almost never served at a formal dinner or in an upscale restaurant. But even at a picnic, a gentleman butters his corn carefully. He spreads the butter along a couple of rows of kernels and then picks up the ear, using both hands. He bites off the kernels, working from one end of the ear to the other. He then butters another couple of rows and proceeds in the same fashion.

Crab: To get the maximum amount of meat, and the maximum pleasure, from a crab, a gentleman first uses his fingers to tear off the legs. Then, making as little noise as possible, he sucks out the meat. Next, he breaks open the back (a small hammer may be provided for this purpose; otherwise, he uses his knife and fork) and removes the meat with his fork. (If he is lucky, a small fork will have been provided for this purpose; otherwise, he uses his dinner fork and the tip of his knife.) A soft-shell crab is entirely edible, and may be eaten with a knife and fork.

Escargot: If a gentleman encounters escargot (the French term for edible snails) at a dinner party, he will be provided with the equipment necessary for eating them. A special pair of tongs to grip the snail and a small fork for pulling the meat out of the shell will be provided. The tiny shellfish fork is placed on the right side of the plate, outside the knife and spoon. If no tongs are provided, the gentleman must use his fingers to hold the shell. He makes sure to get a good grip. Otherwise, the rounded shells may go sailing around the room.

French fries: In a casual setting, a gentleman simply picks his french fries up with his fingers, or he may choose to use a fork. He attempts not to slather his fries with ketchup or other sauces, lest he dribble the sauce on the table or on himself. If the fry is too large to be consumed in a single bite, the gentleman does not put the half-eaten piece back on his plate. Instead, he keeps it in his fingers or on his fork until he is ready to eat it. If a gentleman and other diners are sharing a dipping sauce, he pours a small pool of the sauce on his plate, replenishing it as the need arises. He does not dip his fries into the communal sauce bowl after every bite. A gentleman does not double dip.

Fried chicken: Although fried chicken is a delicious American classic, a gentleman will rarely encounter it anywhere except in the most informal of settings, such as picnics, at-home dinners, or very casual restaurants. In these settings, it is perfectly correct for him to eat the chicken with his fingers. Using the fingers is, in fact, much more convenient than attempting to cut the meat from the bones with a knife and fork. Whenever he eats anything with his fingers, of course, a gentleman makes frequent use of his napkin. A boneless breast of chicken, either fried, baked, or grilled, is another matter entirely. A gentleman always eats it with his knife and fork.

Grapefruit: If the grapefruit sections have not already been loosened from the rind, a gentleman removes the fruit using a grapefruit spoon, which has a serrated edge, if one is provided. Otherwise, he uses his knife and fork to loosen the sections. He conducts this procedure very carefully, however, to prevent squirting the juice on his fellow diners or on his own shirt. If necessary, a gentleman uses his utensil-free hand, to steady the grapefruit. Once the flesh of the grapefruit has been separated from the rind, he eats it with his grapefruit spoon or with his fork, whichever has been provided.

Grapes: If the grapes are served in clusters, a gentleman picks up the cluster and eats the grapes with his fingers. If the grapes are removed from the cluster and served as a garnish, he may eat them with his fingers or spear them with his fork. If the grapes are part of a fruit salad, he always uses a fork.

Gravy: If a gravy or sauce is served along with any course, a gentleman serves himself, using the ladle or spoon accompanying the bowl or gravy boat. He pours the gravy or sauce directly on the food for which it was intended. He does not use it to drown everything served on his plate.

Lemon or lime: A gentleman will often be offered lemon, either cut in half or served as wedges, to accompany beverages, seafood, or vegetables. At some dinners, and at many restaurants, a lemon half will arrive tied up in a piece of fine-mesh fabric. This "bootee" is intended to prevent lemon seeds from splattering over the gentleman's food or onto the plates of his fellow diners. In any case, whether he is squeezing lemon into his iced tea or over his salmon steak, a gentleman squeezes it with one hand, using the other hand to shield himself and others from the spray of citrus juice.

Lobster: A delicacy for some, lobster can also be a disaster if a gentleman does not know how to handle it. Because eating lobster can be an extremely messy ritual, it is one time when a gentleman may protect his shirtfront by stuffing his napkin into his collar. In some restaurants, he may even be offered a bib. Here is the technique for attacking a succulent lobster:

1. Twist off the claws. Separate the sections of the front claws at each of the joints.

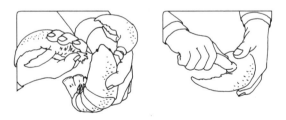

2. Crack the claws with nutcrackers (which will be provided in restaurants or homes where lobster is served). Use a pick, as needed, to remove the flesh from the claws.

3. Twist the tail from the body.

4. Remove the tail flippers from the tail.

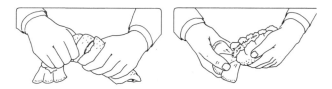

5. Using a fork, push out the tail meat.

6. Remove the shell from the body of the lobster.

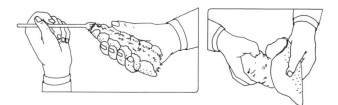

7. Remove the smaller claws.

8. Using a pick, a fork, or even your teeth, remove the meat from the smaller claws.

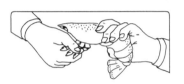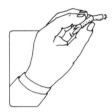

Melon, served in the rind: A gentleman uses his knife and fork to eat any melon that is served in its rind—whether it is watermelon, cantaloupe, honeydew, or any other variety. He makes vertical cuts in the flesh of the melon, slicing almost down to the rind. He then slices across the upper edge of the fruit, thus cutting it into bite-sized cubes that may be tidily eaten, using his fork. If the melon has already been cubed, the gentleman simply eats it with his fork.

Oysters, clams, and other mollusks, served on the half shell: A gentleman firmly grips the shell in one hand and, using his cocktail or oyster fork, spears the delicious morsel. If he wishes, he dips it into any sauce that is provided. A gentleman eats any oyster, clam, mussel, or other mollusk in one bite. In an informal setting—such as an oyster bar or a party among close friends—he may pick up the shell and sip the juice, known as the "liquor."

Pasta: When faced with a plate of pasta, a gentleman resists every temptation to chop it up with his knife and fork. Instead, using the bowl of his spoon for assistance, if necessary, he twirls a manageable mouthful around the tines of his fork and transfers it to his mouth.

Pineapple: When a gentleman is served pineapple, it will most often be cut into rings or wedges, which he cuts into bite-sized pieces, using his fork (and his knife, if the fruit is tough). If the pineapple is served in its skin, however, he eats it in the same way he would eat a melon such as cantaloupe (see *Melon*).

Pizza: Pizza is one of the world's most informal, and potentially messy, foods. In most instances, in fact, a gentleman is expected to pick up an appealing slice and eat it using his fingers. If he finds that the pizza is still piping hot from the oven, and thus too hot to handle, or if it is loaded with messy, albeit tasty, toppings, he may wish to use a knife and fork. That decision, however, is entirely his own and is not dependent upon the behavior of anyone else at the table.

Quail and other small birds: A gentleman uses his knife and fork to slice off and eat as much meat as possible from the bird. Since some meat will inevitably remain on the bones, he may pick them up and tear away the tasty morsels with his teeth. He does so discreetly, however, avoiding any sucking noises.

Quesadillas: If the quesadilla is cooked in butter and is still warm and greasy, a gentleman eats it with his knife and fork. If it is served at room temperature and the grease is unlikely to ooze onto the table or his shirtfront, he may use his fingers to pick up a slice of the quesadilla. In either case, however, he keeps his napkin handy.

Sandwiches: In most cases, a gentleman eats a sandwich in the traditional way, using both hands. An open-faced sandwich or an extremely large, messy sandwich, such as a double-decker burger, may require that he resort to a knife and fork.

Shish kabob: To eat a shish kabob, a gentleman begins by picking up the skewer and using his dinner fork (not his fingers) to slide all the cubes of meat or vegetables onto his plate. He places the used skewer on the rim of his plate and uses his knife and fork to eat the meat and vegetables.

Steaks or chops: A gentleman uses his knife and fork to cut the meat into bite-sized pieces, cutting off one bite-sized morsel at a time. (He does not slice up the entire steak or chop before beginning to eat.) In the case of small, slender chops, such as the bone-in chops from rack of lamb, he does his best to cut the meat away from the bone, one bite at a time. Almost invariably, however, he will find that a good bit of meat will remain on the bone. At that point, he feels free to pick up the bone and tear away the meat, using his teeth, although he avoids making any unpleasant noises. A gentleman never picks up the bone from a sizable steak or chop.

Strawberries: If served on a plate or in a bowl, sliced and with the hulls removed, a gentleman eats strawberries with his fork or spoon. If served with the hull still attached, whether the berry is fresh from the garden or dipped in chocolate, a gentleman simply uses his fingers to remove the hull, discards it on his plate, and pops the berry into his mouth.

Sushi: When eating sushi, a gentleman may use either chopsticks or his fingers. If he does use his fingers, however, he makes sure to wash his hands thoroughly after the meal in order to rinse away any fishy smell.

To eat sushi with chopsticks:

1. Using the chopsticks, gently grip the sushi lengthwise, so the rice does not fall apart.

2. If you wish, gently dip the sushi, rice side down, in soy sauce or any other sauce that may be provided.

3. Bring the sushi to your mouth. (Sushi is intended to be eaten in one or two bites, one bite after the other. A gentleman does not return half-eaten sushi to his plate.)

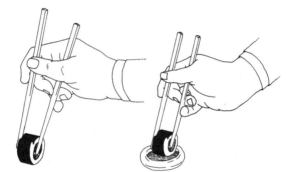

To eat sushi with your fingers, pick it up carefully, using your thumb and middle finger, then proceed as if you were using chopsticks.

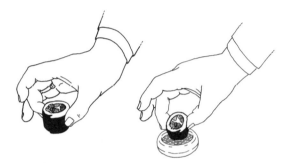

3

SERVING AND BEING SERVED

A GENTLEMAN AT A PRIVATE DINNER

A single man living alone may find it convenient to eat over the sink, or to eat from paper plates or whatever container his take-out comes in, but at times a gentleman will want to have friends or family over so that he can enjoy their company in his own home. Needless to say, he will find it much easier to rise to those occasions if he practices good table manners at every meal, even when he is the only person watching.

When he is hosting a meal for guests, a gentleman takes pains to be on his absolute best behavior. When he is seated at the head of his own table, he takes special care not to let his manners slip.

When a gentleman is entertaining
at home, he turns off the television,
unless the purpose of the party is to
watch a television program, such as a
ball game or a concert.

––––––

If a gentleman chooses
to play background music during a
dinner party, he makes sure it stays in
the background so that it does not
overwhelm the table conversation.

––––––

A gentleman never comes
to the table without his shirt.

––––––

If a gentleman discovers that
he is running as much as fifteen
minutes late for a dinner party or for
cocktails, either in a private home or
in a restaurant, he makes every
attempt to contact his host or
hostess, urging that the party go
ahead without him.

––––––

Even if he is not
a praying person, when grace is
said or a prayer of blessing is offered
at any meal, a gentleman bows his
head. He need not feel compelled
to say "amen," however, unless
he wishes to do so.

———

A gentleman never argues
with friends at the table.

———

In the midst of
a dinner conversation—or in any
conversation—a gentleman does not
attempt to make himself the
center of attention.

———

A gentleman does not
reach or grab for food. Instead, he
waits for it to be passed to him by
a fellow diner, or to be served
to him by a server.

———

If a gentleman desires
a second helping from any dish on
the table, once everyone at the table
has been served, he does not refrain
from asking, "Would you please pass
the dressing?" "Might I have some
more gravy?" or "I think I'd like a
little more of the stroganoff. Would
you please pass it my way?"

———

A gentleman does not
wash down his food with great gulps
of water, or any other beverage.

———

A gentleman does not salt his
food before tasting it.

———

If a gentleman does not find an
ashtray beside his place at the dinner
table, he does not ask for one.

———

A gentleman does not
"eat and run."

———

Unless he has been rudely served, in the extreme, a gentleman never corrects the behavior of a server at a private dinner party, as he understands that that person is the employee of his host or hostess.

———

As soon as his host or hostess shuts down the bar or turns off the coffeepot, a gentleman knows it is time to go home.

———

No matter how informal the event at which he has been entertained, a gentleman always says thank you, either in writing or by telephone.

———

A gentleman knows that the written thank-you note never goes out of style.

———

Dinner Is Served

If a gentleman attends even a few dinner parties, he will discover that his food may be served to him in a variety of ways. Almost all varieties of service, however, are based on one of three traditions.

English service: This service, also referred to as "family service," is the one most familiar to gentlemen. The serving dishes are brought to the table by the host or hostess, and then passed from one guest to another. It is unnecessary for the host or hostess ever to leave the table, except to refill the water pitcher or breadbasket, or to offer second helpings of the main course or side dishes if the serving dishes have been removed to a sideboard or returned to the kitchen.

Russian service: This service, also known as "banquet service," is considerably more formal than English service. In this system, servers arrange the food on the plates and then set them in front of the guests, or bring the serving dishes around, allowing each guest to serve himself or herself. Russian service, or a version thereof, is the service provided at almost all restaurants and at almost every formal banquet, whether a fund-raiser or a rehearsal dinner.

Mixed service: In this service, the main course and its side dishes may be presented on serving dishes at the table so that the guests may serve themselves or be served by the host or hostess. Soup, salad, and dessert, arranged on individual plates, may be served directly from the kitchen.

In any case, it is not a gentleman's responsibility to define the manner in which his food is served to him. Instead, he simply eats what is put in front of him, as it is presented.

When a gentleman hosts a dinner party in his own home, however, it is his responsibility to decide how the meal will be served and to plan accordingly. He takes into account such factors as the formality of the evening, the size of his dining table (a small table may not be able to comfortably accommodate several serving dishes), and his desire to hire a server. Whatever choices he has made, a gentleman host serves dinner as follows:

- The host announces that dinner is ready and invites the guests to the table, showing them to their places.
- If he is serving a salad, the host places the salad plates directly on the dinner plates (which have already been set).
- When the guests have finished their salads, the host removes the salad plates. If he plans to serve the dinner plates in the kitchen, he takes them away at the same time. The salad forks are cleared away with the salad plates.

- The host either serves the dinner plates in the kitchen, or he brings the main course and its side dishes to the table, where the guests serve themselves.
- The host may wish to fill his guests' wine glasses for the first time himself. From then on, at an intimate gathering of friends, he encourages them to serve themselves, passing the bottle from person to person.
- When his guests have finished the main course, with second helpings if they are offered, the host clears away the dinner plates along with the dinner forks and knives.
- Salad may follow the entrée, if the host prefers.
- Finally, the host serves dessert. If he has not already placed the dessert forks or spoons on the table, he may bring them out along with the dessert itself. If there is coffee, he serves it now.

On the Home Vine

When a gentleman entertains in his own home, he selects the wines that complement the dinner he is offering. He knows what he will be serving for the salad or fish course, so he chooses a wine that goes well with that course. To accompany his main course, he serves an appropriate wine of his own choosing, as if it were part of the entrée (which it is). If a guest is unhappy with the wine he has been served, and unless the gentleman has a considerable wine cellar, the host simply says to the guest, "I'm afraid that's the only suitable wine we have on hand. Would you prefer water or soda?"

Even if a gentleman maintains a fine wine cellar, he does not break into it simply to indulge the tastes of whimsical friends.

About Flowers and Candles

When a gentleman hosts a romantic dinner for two in his own home, fresh flowers and the soft glow of candles enhance his table. But the flowers need to be an asset to the table, not an obstruction. He arranges them in a low vase or bowl, so they don't prevent him from making eye contact with his guest. A gentleman shies away from overly aromatic blooms such as heavy-scented lilies, which can overpower even the strongest passion.

Candlelight makes anybody look more attractive, including the gentleman himself. As with flowers, candles should be positioned so that they are not an obstacle or a safety hazard. The gentleman lights them just before serving the salad course, and he makes sure to snuff them out before leaving the table. (When snuffing out candles, he cups one hand behind the flame, to prevent hot wax from spattering across the table and onto his guest.)

In order to make sure that his candles can be easily lit, a clever host tests them ahead of time, letting them burn for a few minutes so that some of the wax slides away from the wick.

DINING AT ITS MOST CASUAL

Although a gentleman may occasionally be invited to formal dinners, complete with white linen, a panoply of flatware, and a steady parade of dishes and wine glasses, he will more often be included in at-home dinners of a much more informal sort. These days, in fact, many homes are designed with spacious dens or television rooms or even with kitchens that are large enough for entertaining a medium-sized dinner party.

Even in the most casual of circumstances, however, a gentleman does not forget his manners. He makes careful use of his napkin, and he attempts to avoid dropping his flatware or spilling gravy on the floor, even if it is sealed in stain-resistant polymers.

At parties such as this—whether the occasion is a birthday, a holiday, or simply the camaraderie of long-time friends—a gentleman may have an opportunity to pitch in with the last-minute preparation of the meal. He may be asked to toss the salad, to fill the water glasses, or to open the wine. At the end of the meal, he may even offer to help collect the dirty dishes, but he does not take it upon himself to provide assistance of any sort if his host or hostess has declined his offer. Only if he is an extremely intimate friend of the host or hostess—and only then if he is the last guest remaining—does he offer to help wash the dishes. No matter how good his intentions might be, a gentleman does not run the risk of embarrassing other guests, who may feel pressured to join in the cleanup party.

Once his host or hostess has said, "Thank you for the offer, Phil, but I'll just straighten these things up a little later," a gentleman does not force the issue. In this situation, as in every other situation, a gentleman knows how to take no for an answer.

Table Talk

When he is the host or a guest at any gathering, a gentleman does his best to make pleasant conversation, both for his own enjoyment and for the enjoyment of others. If he is among strangers or persons with whom he is not well acquainted, he always begins by introducing himself to the guest or guests standing or seated closest to him. If it seems necessary, he then introduces those guests to one another.

A gentleman may attempt to begin the conversation with the most innocuous of icebreakers, such as "Mary Jo certainly sets a lovely table, doesn't she?" or "Jim and Jack's garden really looks great this time of year, doesn't it?" In no case does he ask prying or personal questions. He may ask, "Are you from here in Topeka?" as that question allows his new friend to share as much personal information as he or she cares to divulge. He does not, however, begin the conversation by asking,

"Now, just how is it that you know Mary Jo and Hiram?" (The guest, after all, may have been the doctor who cared for Hiram's recently deceased father, in which case the gentleman may find himself and his fellow guest involved in an unhappy topic.) Similarly, a gentleman does not open the conversation by asking, "And just what is it you do for a living, Morris?" as that question may imply that the gentleman considers his fellow guest's job to be the only thing interesting about his or her life. And in times of economic distress, it can be awkward for the guest who happens to be unhappily unemployed.

If a gentleman is seated next to a lady, he may open the conversation by paying her an unobtrusive compliment, such as "That's a very beautiful brooch." He hopes, of course, that she will respond by saying something that will advance the conversation, such as, "Thank you. It's been in the family for years," or "Thank you, I'm fond of it too. Thomas, my husband, gave it to me as a souvenir of our trip to Bangkok."

A gentleman makes every effort to engage in conversation with both of the guests seated next to him. A longstanding rule of etiquette demands that he switch from one dinner partner to the other every time a new course is brought to the table. Such rigid obedience to rules is no longer expected or required: A gentleman need not break off an interesting discussion with the person on his right, or interrupt the conversation of the person on his left, simply because the salad course has arrived.

At a dinner table of any size, or in a crowded, noisy dining room, a gentleman does not attempt to engage the entire table in his conversation. Instead, he converses quietly with the people seated nearest to him. A gentleman never shouts at a dinner party.

Whether he is seated between strangers or next to his closest friends, a gentleman always steers away from potentially controversial subjects—which means that he avoids the topics of politics or religion at almost any cost.

Should his dinner companion attempt to raise such topics, the gentleman does his best to change the subject. If he must do so, he simply says, "I'd prefer not to talk about that right now," and without letting the pace of the conversation lag, he proceeds by asking, "Have you seen the new Monica Maxwell movie? I think she's always a lot of fun."

FRAGILE—HANDLE WITH CARE

Even the most graceful, meticulous gentleman has his clumsy moments. While enjoying drinks before dinner, he may nudge a vase from an end table; during dinner, he may cause a wine goblet to slide off the table. He may send a cocktail glass shattering to the floor at any time.

In such cases, a gentleman's only immediate recourse is to say, "I'm sorry. May I help clean up?"

Under no circumstances does a gentleman attempt to offer his host monetary compensation for the destroyed property. Instead, he attempts to replace it. (Of course, he does not attempt to replicate a family heirloom or find a substitute for a precious antique.) In any case, a gentleman sends his thank-you note for the party, including a reiteration of his apology, as soon as possible. Even in such situations, however, a gentleman does not grovel. He understands that, over the course of life, things get broken. He says "I'm sorry" as sincerely as possible. Then he moves on.

THE BUCK STOPS HERE

A gentleman does not offer to tip the bartenders or other servers at a private dinner party—even if it is a stand-up cocktail party where the gentleman's glass has been kept filled, repeatedly, by a watchful server. Neither does he attempt to tip the person who helps him with his hat and overcoat. His assumption is that these helpful people will be paid and tipped at the end of the evening by his host or hostess.

The only exception to this rule is an occasion on which a gentleman has been offered some extraordinary kindness or unusual assistance. For example, a gentleman may need to ask a server for help if he discovers that the zipper of his trousers has come loose, he loses a shirt button, or he finds himself feeling ill. In such circumstances he may rightfully offer the helpful server a few folded bills as an expression of his gratitude. He does this by simply passing the bills along to the friendly server, as part of a handshake. Especially in cases such as these, he never neglects to say thank you.

At some public events, such as charity fundraisers—even those with an open bar—a gentleman may notice that the bartender has set up a "tip glass," with a few dollar bills already stuffed in to prime the pump. The tip glass may even be discreetly sequestered behind the bar, but not so discreetly that the gentleman does not see it. In such situations, a gentleman may choose to tip, or not to tip, as he pleases. If he expects to return to that bartender at any point in the evening, however, the gentleman will probably choose to tip, at least a dollar each time he visits the bar.

In all circumstances, a gentleman does, however, take it upon himself to tip valet parkers, if that service is provided. He tips the driver who brings his car around to him. At a party in a private home, a tip of two dollars will usually suffice. In a large city, especially at a restaurant, a gentleman may wish to tip as much as five dollars. If a gentleman only has a lone dollar bill in his wallet, however, he pushes it into the valet's hand, slips behind the wheel of his car, and sails off into the night.

RESPONDING TO INVITATIONS

When he has been invited to dinner, a gentleman always responds promptly, whether he must accept or regret. If his plans change for an unforeseen and unavoidable reason, he again notifies his host or hostess as quickly as possible.

When he receives a dinner invitation from a married couple, a gentleman sends his acceptance or his regrets to his would-be hostess.

When a gentleman receives a dinner invitation from an unmarried couple, he sends his acceptance or his regrets to both of his would-be hosts or hostesses. On the envelope he lists their names in alphabetical order according to their last names, and on the enclosed note of acceptance or regrets he writes their first names, also in alphabetical order.

If a gentleman has been entertained at dinner, he always says thank you, either at the moment, by phone the next day, or by a note, mailed within the next forty-eight hours.

When a gentleman has been entertained by a married couple, he sends his thank-you note to his hostess. He may express his gratitude to both his host and his hostess, but tradition assumes that it is his hostess who has thrown the party, and it is to her that his thank-you should be addressed.

When a gentleman has been entertained by an unmarried couple, he follows the same procedure with his thank-you note as with his response note. He addresses it to both people, listing their names in alphabetical order by last name on the envelope, and their first names in alphabetical order on the enclosed thank-you note.

THE UNINVITED GUEST

If a gentleman has been brought to a party to which he has not specifically been invited and discovers that the party is a seated dinner with no room for him, he does not expect his host or hostess to set a place for him. Instead, he leaves immediately, realizing that there may not be enough food or flatware to accommodate him. It is not inappropriate for him to ask the friend who brought him to the party to drive him home. Or he may call a cab. In such circumstances he does the best he can to prevent inconveniencing or embarrassing the host or hostess. He exits as quickly and as graciously as possible, saying, "So sorry for the misunderstanding. I hope we can get together some time soon." In such situations, it is not the gentleman's responsibility to write a note of apology. That responsibility lies with the person who brought him, without warning, to the dinner.

4

IN THE PRESENCE OF OTHERS

DINING AT A RESTAURANT

Although many of the same rules apply as if he were dining in a private home—after all, a table is a table—when a gentleman is dining in a restaurant, some situations arise that are unique to that public world. Not only is he in the company of his own dinner partner (or partners), but he is also in a room surrounded by many other diners, each of whom is hoping to enjoy a pleasant meal. However, a gentleman need not be intimidated by such situations, no matter how elegant the décor or the clientele. From choosing wine to pronouncing an unfamiliar word on a menu, a gentleman can learn how to maneuver in a restaurant, enabling him to start out the evening with an advantage.

Unless his host or hostess
lights up first, or he is in the absolute
privacy of his own home or in the
smoking section of a restaurant,
a gentleman never smokes
at the table.

————

Unless he is in a designated
"cigar-friendly" establishment or
household, a gentleman does not
light up a cigar in any place where
others are eating.

————

If a gentleman feels that
he must light up a cigarette or a
cigar in a restaurant and his table is in
the no-smoking section, he heads for
the bar—knowing full well that he
may discover restrictions against
cigar smoking, even there.

————

Whenever a gentleman
heads out for a night on the town,
whether as the host or a guest for
the evening, he makes sure to carry a
supply of dollar bills so that he is
ready to tip valet parkers, doormen,
and washroom attendants whenever
the need arises.

———

In a restaurant, if a gentleman
wants a steak knife, he asks for one,
saying "Thank you very much" when
it has been provided.

———

A gentleman assumes that his
food will be served to him from the
left, and that his empty dishes will be
cleared away from the right.

———

If a gentleman is asked to offer a
toast—or if he chooses to offer one,
of his own accord—he keeps it brief,
tasteful, and to the point.

———

A gentleman says please and thank you, especially to servers—either in a restaurant or in a private home.

———

If another diner asks to sample a gentleman's food and the gentleman is willing to oblige, he may respond by asking his fellow diner to lend the gentleman his or her fork and bread plate, so the gentleman can offer a couple of mouthfuls of the requested dish.

———

If a gentleman truly finds it unpleasant or awkward to share his food with others, he simply declines the request, saying, "Everybody's food looks so delicious. Let's just stick to our own plates, if you don't mind."

———

For his own part, however, under no circumstances does a gentleman ask to taste another person's food.

———

When he is expected to pay for his own meal in a restaurant, a gentleman is not ashamed to ask the price of any special item offered by the server.

————

Should the diners at a table close to his own become so boisterous as to imperil the pleasure of the gentleman's own dinner companions, he does not attempt to chasten them. Instead, he leaves his table to seek the assistance of the maître d', the host, or the hostess.

————

When dining in a restaurant, a gentleman feels free to ask for a "doggie bag" or a "to-go box."

————

If a gentleman knows the first name of any server in a restaurant, he feels free to use it.

————

GATHERINGS IN RESTAURANTS

More and more often, when it comes to entertaining, a gentleman finds himself at a restaurant, whether he is the host or a guest. The occasion may be a business meal, a simple gathering of friends, or the celebration of a birthday, an anniversary, or some other milestone.

No matter what the reason for the dinner, a gentleman knows that his behavior in a public place may be scrutinized even more closely than at a private party.

The Gentleman as Host

When a gentleman intends to host a dinner for friends at a restaurant, he always makes it clear whether he is paying the entire bill or whether each person is expected to pay his or her share. He may say, "I hope you and Jenny will be my guests for dinner at the Gewgaw Club on Saturday night." Alternatively, if the gentleman merely intends to bring together a group of friends, each of whom is expected to pay his or her own way for the evening, he may say, "I was wondering if you and Paolo would be available for dinner on Friday night. I was thinking we'd stop in at Loco Coco, around eight—very casual, dutch treat."

If the gentleman's invitation is accepted, he makes sure that his guests know the time of the dinner reservation, the address and phone number of the restaurant, and any dress code that is required for the gentlemen in the party. Fewer and fewer restaurants require that a gentleman wear a coat and tie, even for dinner, but such requirements do persist in some establishments, and a host is always wise to ask ahead of time rather than risk embarrassing one of his guests. If there is a dress code for gentlemen, it may also give his lady guests some indication as to how they may choose to dress for the evening.

In choosing a restaurant at which to entertain

his friends or business clients, a gentleman does his best to select an establishment where everyone at the table can make a happy choice from the menu. In most restaurants nowadays, the menu includes at least one vegetarian selection, but a gentleman takes extra precautions before inviting his friends to an ethnic restaurant or one that is noted for its unusual cuisine. His best course is to be straightforward, saying, "A group of us are going to that wonderful Thai restaurant on Mobberly Road." If his guest is not fond of Thai cuisine, the gentleman may elect to suggest another restaurant. If the host has made it clear that a group of friends are involved in the party—which is what he should do—the well-mannered invitee will say, "I think I'll take a pass this time. Thai doesn't settle well with me. I hope you'll give me a rain check."

If several other friends have already accepted the gentleman's invitation, it will be difficult for him to rearrange the entire excursion, although he may be willing to go beyond the call of duty to do so. Meanwhile, if the Thai-negative friend is the first to be asked, the host will find it easy to adjust his plans. In either case, once the host has revamped the evening to accommodate the guest's preferences, the guest must accept the invitation and do his best to be a glad participant in the dinner party.

A gentleman does his best to arrive at the restaurant ahead of, or at least along with, his guests so that he can claim the reservation and make sure his guests are not left lingering in the foyer or at the bar. If there is a delay before his party is seated, his guests may choose to have a drink at the bar. If he is paying for the entire dinner, the host picks up the bar tab, as well, leaving an appropriate tip for the bartender. It is not bad form for a guest to offer to pay for a round of drinks. A host may accept or decline the offer, as he chooses.

When his party's table is ready, the host may choose to dictate who sits next to whom. If the occasion is purely social, he seats his guests in the same way he would seat them in his own home. If the occasion is a business meal, he seats his guests in an arrangement that expedites the work to be done.

In most restaurants a server will appear, almost immediately, to fill the party's water glasses and ask if anybody would like anything else to drink. The guests may, of course, order anything they please, whether it is a cocktail, wine or beer, iced tea, or a soda. When the server returns with the drinks, he or she may inform the party of any "specials" available that evening but not included on the printed menu. If the guests have questions, they ask them, particularly if they are concerned about food allergies or carbohydrate intake. Any guest may simply ask, "Does the spinach salad have nuts in it?" or "Is it possible for me to get the Sunrise Pasta *without* the shrimp?"

The server may recommend appetizers, but they need not be ordered if the diners have no interest in them. The host may choose to tell the waiter, "We'd like a few minutes, please." All the guests then turn their focus to the menu so they can be ready to order when the server returns. The host does not hurry his guests along; the guests themselves, however, do their best to keep the dinner running on a smooth schedule.

If the gentleman wants to steer his friends away from the more expensive cuisine, he may suggest to his friends, "I understand the grilled salmon is delicious." (On the other hand, a gentleman always checks out the prices at any restaurant before he invites friends or clients to dine there on his tab.) If a guest chooses instead to order the filet mignon, the gentleman host does not flinch.

After all his guests have finished their entrées, desserts, after-dinner drinks, and coffee, a gentleman may ask for the bill. His guests may offer to pitch in to help pay the tab, but if he invited them as guests, he simply says, "No, thank you. You're my guests for the evening."

Once the gentleman has made it clear, *ahead of time*, that everybody is to pay his or her own way, he requests in advance that the server provide separate checks. (At a party where nobody is clearly the "host," it is appropriate for anybody at the table to request separate checks.) If the restaurant has a no-separate-checks policy, and if everybody's bill seems to be approximately the same, and if all his fellow diners approve, he may ask the server simply to split the bill equally among the guests, or among the couples, as the case may be.

A gentleman does his best to make sure his guests know that the party is going dutch. Unless he is already familiar with the restaurant, he calls ahead to ask if separate checks are offered. If he is told that the restaurant has a no-separate-checks policy, he passes that information along to the other people in his group, so that they can bring along cash to pitch in when it comes time for the gentleman to coordinate the payment of the bill. (And, if he has extended the invitation, it *will* be his responsibility to make sure the bill has been paid, with an appropriate tip added in, at the end of the evening, although it may require his asking, "Does anybody have a couple more dollars for the tip?") Even without requesting a separate check, a guest may attempt to pay his portion of the bill with a credit card, simply asking, "Would you please put fifty dollars on this card?" Nevertheless, some restaurants refuse to make even this concession.

In such situations, the host is faced with the challenge of being fair to everyone at the table, but he also does his best to be fair to himself, in hopes that he will not be left paying an inordinate share of the bill. He may decree, "It looks like everybody's share, tip included, is fifty dollars." Or he may take the risk of suggesting, "Everybody pitch in whatever seems right." The latter option certainly demonstrates consideration for the guest who only drank iced tea and ordered the chicken sandwich, but it also leaves the gentleman vulnerable to the undependable generosity and sobriety, or even the honesty, of his fellow guests. He may be wiser to propose, "Each person's share is fifty dollars. Is that OK with everybody?" Given that option, the guest who's eaten modestly has every right to say, "If it's all right with you, I believe my share is more like twenty dollars." It is the guest's responsibility to contribute a fair share of the bill, remembering to cover his or her share of the tip. It is the gentleman's responsibility to say, "Sure, Gus. That sounds fine."

If there is only one check, it is the gentleman's responsibility to determine the server's tip and to include it in the shared total for the evening. If a tip for the wine steward or the maître d' is requested, the gentleman includes it in the shared total.

The Gentleman as Guest

If a gentleman is invited for dinner in a restaurant, either as a friend or a business colleague, he accepts or declines the invitation as soon as possible. If the invitation is to a restaurant where he knows he does not like or cannot eat the food, he states that fact clearly. Without further elaboration, he says, "You're kind to invite me, Bob, but the menu at Middle Europa doesn't work very well for me." If the intent of the luncheon or the dinner is to do business, and if the gentleman's opinion is asked, he says, "Middle Europa doesn't work well for me. Can we choose some other place?"

If a gentleman is fortunate, the friend who invited him to dinner will have made his intentions as clear as possible regarding who is paying the bill. The thoughtful host will have avoided any confusion by saying either, "I hope you'll be my guest next Friday evening at the Rossland House," or "Are you available for dinner at the Rossland House next Friday? It'll be dutch treat. I think we'll have a good time."

If the gentleman knows that the Rossland House is beyond his price range and the dinner is to be dutch treat (or if the host has left him uncertain as to who will pay), the gentleman simply says, "Thanks so much, Bob, but I'm afraid I already have an engagement for Friday night. I wish I could join you, but maybe we can grab a drink sometime soon." This is as much explanation as a gentleman need offer when declining any invitation. If a gentleman's wallet decrees that he cannot afford to accept Bob's invitation, his safest course is to stay home or to bring together a group of other friends for an evening of burgers and fries at a more moderately priced restaurant. All the while, he remains fully confident that, before long, the Rossland House will be within his budget. He does not overextend himself now, however, simply to keep up with more affluent friends.

If Joe is available to accept Bob's invitation, he does his best to help make the evening a success. If he and other diners have enjoyed drinks at the bar before they are seated at their table, he may offer to pay the bar tab. In no case does he argue with his host, however. He may say, "Please, let me do this," but if the host declines the offer, he drops the issue.

At the table, the gentleman guest sits where he is told to sit, helps the lady next to him with her chair, and makes conversation with his dinner companions, just as if he were at a private dinner. When it comes to ordering his dinner, if separate checks are not available, he attempts to order in the same price range as his fellow diners so as to avoid inequities when the check is split at the end of the evening. In such situations, if everybody else is ordering fish or chicken, he does not order steak.

If a gentleman has eaten less expensively than others in the party, he offers to pay his fair share (a gentleman does not forget to include a tip) when it comes time to divide the bill. Again, if a gentleman feels awkward about speaking up on his own behalf, and if he knows that his fellow diners are big spenders, he does not diminish his enjoyment of the evening by worrying about how much he will have to pay. If such are his fears, he declines the invitation.

If the host has ordered wine for the table, and if the gentleman is a teetotaler, and if it is not an assault on his personal morality, he may still choose to pay an equal share of the bill. The cost of fine wine can be prohibitive, however, and the nondrinking gentleman need not feel obliged to help in paying for it. When it comes time to pay the bill, he contributes his fair share. He does not say, "Simon, you know I'm not a drinker, so I'm not going to pay for any of that."

At all times throughout a restaurant dinner, a gentleman attempts to maintain a congenial, businesslike relationship with his server. If he is a guest at the table, and if he feels he is being rudely or ineptly served, he informs his host of that fact, saying, "Horace, I'm really having a problem with this server. He and I simply aren't getting along. Would you mind checking in with the manager?"

Coupon Etiquette

When a gentleman is dining at a restaurant and has a coupon for a discounted meal or a free drink, dessert, or other item, he offers the coupon to his server before he and his fellow diners have begun to order their meal. The server may say, "I'll take the coupon at the end of the meal," but at least he will know to ask for it before totaling the bill. A gentleman does not assume that he will be given inferior service simply because he has offered a discount coupon to pay for part of his meal.

If a gentleman makes use of a discount coupon, or if he has been offered a complimentary item, such as a drink, an appetizer, or a dessert, he leaves his server the same tip he would have provided if he were paying full price He knows that his bill will usually indicate the pre-discount price of the meal. If he must consult a menu to determine the price of the complimentary item, he does so.

Dining at the Bar

From time to time, in a restaurant of virtually any type, a gentleman may choose to take his luncheon or dinner at the bar. He need not drink alcohol to do so. His only assumption—and the only assumption of the bartender—is that he wishes to dine efficiently, with attentive service.

Whether or not he drinks alcohol, a gentleman may establish a congenial relationship with the man or woman behind the bar. The bartender's job is not to push liquor upon customers (the law proscribes this). His or her job is simply to provide congenial, bartenderly service.

If he is an inveterate bar diner, a gentleman may be skilled in striking up conversations—either with the bartender or with other patrons. He is careful at all times, however, not to distract the bartender from his or her job. And, unless a ready opportunity seems to be provided, he is especially careful not to intrude upon the conversations of fellow bar-goers. If he attempts to strike up a conversation with another customer at the bar, and if his fellow customer clearly prefers to dine or drink in peace, a gentleman respects those wishes.

If he has enjoyed his entire dinner at the bar (even if his drink consisted of nothing more than iced tea), when it comes time for tipping, a gentleman remembers the personal attention he has been shown, tipping a minimum of 15 percent for acceptable service, and 20 percent if the bartender has been particularly attentive. It is the gentleman's responsibility to be kind to the bartender when he leaves the place. If he forgets this sort of attention, he should not be surprised that it takes him a great deal longer to get his iced tea the next time he comes to the bar.

THE WELL-FILLED GLASS

If he is hosting a dinner party in a fine restaurant, a gentleman will probably be presented with a wine list. If the gentleman is a connoisseur of wines, he may select them for the entire table. If he is not confident of his own knowledge of wines, he may ask another diner to make the selections. If he is serving as host—and especially if he is paying the bill— he asks that guest to select "something in the $30 to $50 range," or the "$50 to $90 range," whichever he can afford. Even if wine has been ordered by the bottle, he encourages friends to order a glass of any wine they prefer—although wine, by the glass, generally costs considerably more than wine, per glass, from a bottle.

The age-old truism is that white wines go best with chicken or fish, moderately hearty red wines such as Pinot Noir and Zinfandel taste best with pork and lamb, and heavy, spicy reds, such as Cabernet and Shiraz, hold up best against beef. But such rules mean nothing nowadays, when a tuna steak may be every bit as rich as a filet of beef—or when a heavy steak may seem to require something dry, if that's what the diner desires. In short, the host may not be able to find a bottle of wine, or even two bottles of wine, to satisfy the whole table. He may have to pay for individual glasses of wine—and hence may have to pay a great deal more money when it comes time to pay the bill.

When the bottle of wine is brought to the table, it will be presented to the gentleman or lady who ordered it—whether or not that person is the host. (If the wine is presented to the host, and he did not select it, he asks the server to present it to the guest who selected it.) In any case, somebody must inspect the label on the wine bottle to make sure the wine is actually the wine that was ordered.

When the server (in a fine restaurant it will be the wine steward, or *sommelier*), brings the wine to the table, it will be uncorked in the presence of the host or whoever selected it. The server will then offer the cork to the person who selected the wine. The intent of this ritual is not to allow the guest to sniff the cork, to see whether it smells appetizing. Instead, the guest is expected to test the cork, squeezing it lightly to see if it is dried out. If the cork feels dry, the tester may expect the wine to taste inordinately acidic, and he may request an alternative selection.

White wines may be opened close to the time they are to be served, and should be kept cold but not chilled. Red wines, however, should be ordered as soon as it has been determined that red wine will be desired by any of the diners. This is so the bottles can be opened and allowed to "breathe" before they are served.

How to Make a Toast

Over the course of his life, a gentleman will probably be invited to any number of wedding receptions, anniversary dinners, birthday parties, and other events. At some time, almost inevitably, he will be asked to make a toast, and if he is asked, he must not refuse. However, he need not attempt to give an after-dinner speech or perform a comedy routine. His tribute may be something as simple as "Joe, I'm proud to call you my friend."

He may choose to share some memory of his friendship with the honoree, or if he is confident of his skill as a humorist, he may toss off a lighthearted quip. In no case does he attempt to embarrass the guest of honor. Neither does he ramble on at any length. A gentleman remembers that because toasts usually come late in the evening, the wisest course is always to be succinct.

A Fair Percentage

When he serves as host in a restaurant, a gentleman understands that he is responsible for tipping any servers and other staff members who have assisted his party during the luncheon or dinner.

Whether he is paying in cash, on a company account, or with a credit card, a gentleman understands that the minimum standard for a tip—assuming that the table server has provided even acceptable service—is 15 percent of the bill, before tax. A tip of 20 percent is expected for service that is even remotely superior. If a gentleman finds his service to be extraordinary, or even particularly gracious, he may tip even more generously.

In any restaurant, a gentleman may not assume that servers are salaried employees. In many instances, the largest portion of their income comes from their tips, and in many fine restaurants, servers will be expected to share those tips with the busboys, bartenders, and others who help at the gentleman's table. If he has been served well, he does his best to tip fairly.

In many instances at restaurants, when the gentleman is hosting a large party (eight to ten persons or more) the establishment will add a gratuity to the bill. (Eighteen percent is the percentage often added to the total in restaurants nowadays.) A gentleman will find this detail in small print on the menu, and perhaps on the bill as well. (It behooves a gentleman to look closely and use his reading glasses if required—otherwise he may find himself tipping an additional 20 percent on top of the 18 percent already added on.) A gentleman may find this built-in percentage sufficient, or he may wish to add an additional gratuity. (His credit card slip will probably offer him the opportunity to do so, or he may leave additional cash.)

In especially fine restaurants with respectable wine cellars, a gentleman may discover that the bill suggests that he provide a tip for the wine steward, or *sommelier*. If such is the case, and— once again, if the service has been acceptable—a gentleman adds a tip of 15 to 20 percent of the cost of the wine *only*, in gratitude for the wine steward's help.

The gentleman may choose to pay his bill, or leave his tip, in cash. (Many servers prefer cash tips, because cash payment means they do not have to wait for credit card charges to clear the bank.) If he is dining in a fine restaurant with a wine steward, and if he is tipping in cash, a gentleman does not forget to tip the wine steward, and the host of the restaurant, on his way out the door.

In most instances, as the gentleman is exiting, the host or maître d' will approach him with outstretched hand, saying, "I hope you had a lovely evening." If the gentleman expects to receive good service in that restaurant again, he is prepared to shake hands with each of them, slipping a twenty-dollar bill into the handshake. If he has already added a generous tip to his credit card bill, he feels no need to add this extra kindness. Both the steward and the host will be aware of, and will share in, his generosity when the credit card tips are apportioned and sorted out at the end of the evening.

At mid-range restaurants, the sort where most gentlemen dine, such concerns are irrelevant. In most cases the gentleman must simply decide how much he wants to leave for his server, with the server deciding how to split the cash gratuities among the other staff members at the close of the evening.

Under no circumstances is a gentleman intimidated into overtipping for poor service.

He understands that some problems, such as slow service from the bar or the kitchen, are not the table server's fault. If he feels he has been served in a slovenly manner, however, he does not insult his own reputation by leaving a tip of five cents, twenty-five cents, or even five dollars on a sizeable tab. Instead, he leaves nothing at all, but before he leaves the restaurant, he finds the manager or host and explains the reasons for his decision.

Whatever the size of his tip, a gentleman offers it discreetly. After he has added the tip to his credit card slip, he turns it over and either encloses it in the bill cover provided by the restaurant or hands it directly to the server. Under no circumstance does a gentleman brag about or grouse about the size of his tip.

When a gentleman has ordered drinks at the bar before dinner, even if the bartender offers to transfer the bar bill to the gentleman's table, he leaves a gratuity for the bartender as his party moves to its table.

If he visits the bathroom and discovers an attendant there, even if that attendant offers him no particular service, a gentleman is expected to drop a dollar into the attendant's tip basket. He does so each time he stops by the men's room, for whatever reason. The attendant's job is to make sure the men's room is kept clean and well stocked with paper towels and bath tissue. A gentleman should not expect to see such an attendant very often, because even in the largest cities, men's room attendants are infrequently employed, except by upscale restaurants.

When tipping in cash, a gentleman never leaves loose change, unless it is a sizable pocketful of loose change. These days, a tip of less than one dollar is considered no tip at all.

If a gentleman dines at a diner, a breakfast bar, or any other establishment where customers are expected to pay at the cash register, he leaves his tip on the table before heading for the cashier. If he does not have the appropriate amount of cash in his pocket at that moment, he makes sure to ask for change at the cash register, returning to the table, tip in hand, as quickly as possible after paying his bill. If a gentleman uses a credit card to pay his bill at the cash register, he makes sure to add in a tip for his server, just as if he were filling out the credit card slip at the table.

Upon departing the restaurant, a gentleman is prepared to provide the valet parkers with a minimum tip of two dollars—or as much as five dollars, depending on the formality of the restaurant. If a gentleman has only one dollar in his pocket at that late point in the evening, he does not apologize. Instead, he pushes the dollar bill into the parker's hand, saying, "Have a nice evening." A gentleman tries to plan ahead for all eventualities, but occasionally he may have no other option.

On the Menu

Nothing can show more quickly that a gentleman is out of his element than ordering an item off a menu and mispronouncing it—or, worse yet, having it arrive at the table and then realizing that he has just ordered something he does not enjoy or simply cannot eat. These days, a gentleman may find menus filled with items that never turned up on his mother's table. The following list may help a gentleman avoid awkward moments.

WHAT IT SAYS: **al dente**

WHAT IT MEANS: cooked but still firm—not mushy; usually refers to pasta or rice

HOW YOU PRONOUNCE IT: al dent tay

WHAT IT SAYS: **Alfredo**

WHAT IT MEANS: a cream-based sauce served with pasta

HOW YOU PRONOUNCE IT: al fray doh

WHAT IT SAYS: **arugula**

WHAT IT MEANS: a member of the mustard greens family, used primarily in salads

HOW YOU PRONOUNCE IT: ah roo guh lah

WHAT IT SAYS: **Asiago**

WHAT IT MEANS: a hard, pale yellow cheese, usually grated

HOW YOU PRONOUNCE IT: ah zhe ah go

WHAT IT SAYS: **au gratin**

WHAT IT MEANS: covered with bread crumbs or cheese and browned under a broiler

HOW YOU PRONOUNCE IT: oh grah ten

WHAT IT SAYS: **au jus**

WHAT IT MEANS: a method of serving broiled or grilled meat in its natural juices

HOW YOU PRONOUNCE IT: oh zhoo

WHAT IT SAYS: **balsamic vinegar**

WHAT IT MEANS: an aged vinegar made from white grapes, manufactured exclusively in Modena, Italy

HOW YOU PRONOUNCE IT: bal sah mick

WHAT IT SAYS: **basmati**

WHAT IT MEANS: a long-grained brown or white rice

HOW YOU PRONOUNCE IT: bahs mah tee

WHAT IT SAYS: **béarnaise**

WHAT IT MEANS: a smooth-textured sauce made of butter, eggs, shallots, white wine, and vinegar or lemon juice

HOW YOU PRONOUNCE IT: behr nayz

WHAT IT SAYS: **beurre blanc**

WHAT IT MEANS: a hot butter sauce flavored with vinegar or lemon

HOW YOU PRONOUNCE IT: burr blahnk

WHAT IT SAYS: **biscotti**

WHAT IT MEANS: a twice-baked Italian cookie, usually flavored with almonds or anise

HOW YOU PRONOUNCE IT: bee skawt tee

WHAT IT SAYS: **bisque**

WHAT IT MEANS: a thick cream soup often featuring shellfish or a vegetable, such as tomatoes

HOW YOU PRONOUNCE IT: bisk

WHAT IT SAYS: **bleu cheese**

WHAT IT MEANS: a sharp-flavored whitish cheese veined with

blue mold (which gives the cheese its distinctive tang)

How you pronounce it: blue cheese

What it says: **bolognese**

What it means: a style of serving pasta in a sauce made
with tomatoes and ground meat

How you pronounce it: bowl ah naze

What it says: **brioche**

What it means: a sweet French bread made with eggs
and butter

How you pronounce it: bree ohsh

What it says: **bruschetta**

What it means: toasted Italian bread, drizzled with olive
oil, frequently topped with garlic and tomatoes

How you pronounce it: broo skeh tah

What it says: **cacciatore**

What it means: a style of slowly cooking meat or chicken
along with tomatoes, herbs, and sometimes wine

How you pronounce it: kah chuh tor ee

WHAT IT SAYS: **café au lait**

WHAT IT MEANS: strong coffee, mixed in equal parts with steaming hot milk

HOW YOU PRONOUNCE IT: kafay oh lay

WHAT IT SAYS: **calamari**

WHAT IT MEANS: squid

HOW YOU PRONOUNCE IT: kal uh mahr ee

WHAT IT SAYS: **canapé**

WHAT IT MEANS: an hors d'oevure, such as a pâté or other spread, served on a cracker or toast

HOW YOU PRONOUNCE IT: can uh pee

WHAT IT SAYS: **carpaccio**

WHAT IT MEANS: ground or thinly sliced raw meat or fish, served with a sauce

HOW YOU PRONOUNCE IT: kahr pah chee oh

WHAT IT SAYS: **chanterelle**

WHAT IT MEANS: an edible, trumpet-shaped mushroom

HOW YOU PRONOUNCE IT: shan tuh rehl

WHAT IT SAYS: **chipotle**

WHAT IT MEANS: a red chili pepper used in Mexican cuisine

HOW YOU PRONOUNCE IT: chih poht lay

WHAT IT SAYS: **consommé**

WHAT IT MEANS: clear soup made from a well-seasoned beef
or chicken stock

HOW YOU PRONOUNCE IT: kon suh may

WHAT IT SAYS: **cordon bleu**

WHAT IT MEANS: a style of serving meat, usually veal or
chicken, by rolling it around slices of ham and cheese and
coating it in bread crumbs

HOW YOU PRONOUNCE IT: kor dohn bluh

WHAT IT SAYS: **coulis**

WHAT IT MEANS: a simple sauce made with puréed
vegetables or fruit

HOW YOU PRONOUNCE IT: koo lee

WHAT IT SAYS: **couscous**

WHAT IT MEANS: a tiny grain-sized pasta, frequently used in Mediterranean cuisine

HOW YOU PRONOUNCE IT: koos koos

WHAT IT SAYS: **crème brûlée**

WHAT IT MEANS: a custard sprinkled with sugar and then broiled so that the sugar forms a hard-candy topping

HOW YOU PRONOUNCE IT: krehm broo lay

WHAT IT SAYS: **crème caramel**

WHAT IT MEANS: a baked custard topped with caramel

HOW YOU PRONOUNCE IT: krehm kehr ah mehl

WHAT IT SAYS: **crepe**

WHAT IT MEANS: a paper-thin pancake

HOW YOU PRONOUNCE IT: krayp

WHAT IT SAYS: **crepes suzette**

WHAT IT MEANS: crepes warmed in an orange butter sauce and often presented dramatically in a blaze of flaming liquor

HOW YOU PRONOUNCE IT: krayp soo zeht

WHAT IT SAYS: **demi-glace**

WHAT IT MEANS: a concentrated beef-based sauce lightened with consommé

HOW YOU PRONOUNCE IT: dehm ee glahs

WHAT IT SAYS: **demitasse**

WHAT IT MEANS: a small cup of very strong coffee, usually served at the end of a dinner party

HOW YOU PRONOUNCE IT: dehm ee tahss

WHAT IT SAYS: **escargot**

WHAT IT MEANS: edible snails, usually sautéed in butter, sometimes served in their own shells

HOW YOU PRONOUNCE IT: ehs kahr goh

WHAT IT SAYS: **fennel**

WHAT IT MEANS: a licorice-flavored vegetable served either raw in a salad, or as a cooked side dish

HOW YOU PRONOUNCE IT: fehn uhl

WHAT IT SAYS: **feta**

WHAT IT MEANS: a classic Greek curd cheese made with sheep's or goat's milk

HOW YOU PRONOUNCE IT: feht uh

WHAT IT SAYS: **fettuccine**

WHAT IT MEANS: a flat pasta cut into long, thin strips

HOW YOU PRONOUNCE IT: feht tuh chee neh

WHAT IT SAYS: **flan**

WHAT IT MEANS: a simple egg custard, coated with caramel syrup, identical to crème caramel (see *crème caramel*)

HOW YOU PRONOUNCE IT: flahn

WHAT IT SAYS: **focaccia**

WHAT IT MEANS: a flat Italian bread seasoned with herbs and olive oil

HOW YOU PRONOUNCE IT: foe kah chyah

WHAT IT SAYS: **foie gras**

WHAT IT MEANS: the liver of a goose, enriched by force-feeding the bird a diet of rich grains

HOW YOU PRONOUNCE IT: fwah grah

WHAT IT SAYS: **frittata**

WHAT IT MEANS: an unfolded omelet featuring meat and/or vegetables

HOW YOU PRONOUNCE IT: frih tah tuh

WHAT IT SAYS: **ganache**

WHAT IT MEANS: a sweet, creamy chocolate mixture used as a filling or frosting

HOW YOU PRONOUNCE IT: gahn ahsh

WHAT IT SAYS: **génoise**

WHAT IT MEANS: a sponge cake made of butter and stiffly beaten eggs

HOW YOU PRONOUNCE IT: zhayn wahz

WHAT IT SAYS: **gnocchi**

WHAT IT MEANS: a small dumpling made of ground potatoes, broiled or baked, and served with a sauce or grated cheese

HOW YOU PRONOUNCE IT: noh kee

WHAT IT SAYS: **granita**

WHAT IT MEANS: a coarse-textured frozen dessert, usually made with fruit

HOW YOU PRONOUNCE IT: grah nee tah

WHAT IT SAYS: **hollandaise**

WHAT IT MEANS: a sauce made from butter, eggs, and lemon juice

HOW YOU PRONOUNCE IT: hol uhn dayz

WHAT IT SAYS: **hors d'oeuvre**

WHAT IT MEANS: light snacks served at cocktail parties or before a meal

HOW YOU PRONOUNCE IT: or derv

WHAT IT SAYS: **jalapeño**

WHAT IT MEANS: a hot green or red pepper

HOW YOU PRONOUNCE IT: hah lah peh nyoh

WHAT IT SAYS: **Kiev**

WHAT IT MEANS: a classic method of cooking chicken breasts, stuffed with herbs and garlic butter

HOW YOU PRONOUNCE IT: kee ehv

WHAT IT SAYS: **latte**

WHAT IT MEANS: a strong espresso coffee topped with frothy steamed milk

HOW YOU PRONOUNCE IT: lah tay

WHAT IT SAYS: **linguine**

WHAT IT MEANS: a flat pasta cut into long slender strips

HOW YOU PRONOUNCE IT: lihn gwee nee

WHAT IT SAYS: **lyonnaise**

WHAT IT MEANS: a style of seasoning food, using onions and parsley

HOW YOU PRONOUNCE IT: lee uh nayz

WHAT IT SAYS: **marsala**

WHAT IT MEANS: a sweet Italian wine often used to flavor chicken or veal

HOW YOU PRONOUNCE IT: mahr sah lah

WHAT IT SAYS: **Mornay**

WHAT IT MEANS: a thick, velvety cheese sauce

HOW YOU PRONOUNCE IT: mohr nay

WHAT IT SAYS: **mousse**

WHAT IT MEANS: either a frothy chilled dessert, or a light, foamy seafood dish, served cold

HOW YOU PRONOUNCE IT: moose

WHAT IT SAYS: **mousseline**

WHAT IT MEANS: a smooth-textured, delicate sauce to which whipped cream or egg whites have been added

HOW YOU PRONOUNCE IT: moose leen

WHAT IT SAYS: **mussel**

WHAT IT MEANS: a marine or freshwater mollusk, usually steamed with wine

HOW YOU PRONOUNCE IT: muss uhl

WHAT IT SAYS: **niçoise**

WHAT IT MEANS: a style of serving cold vegetables or seafood with tomatoes and olive oil, often including black olives and garlic

HOW YOU PRONOUNCE IT: nee swahz

WHAT IT SAYS: **osso buco**

WHAT IT MEANS: a sliced veal knuckle or shinbone, slow-cooked in olive oil and wine

HOW YOU PRONOUNCE IT: aw soh boo koh

WHAT IT SAYS: **paella**

WHAT IT MEANS: a dish of shellfish, chicken, and rice, flavored with saffron

HOW YOU PRONOUNCE IT: pie ay yuh

WHAT IT SAYS: **pancetta**

WHAT IT MEANS: lean, unsmoked bacon used in Italian cuisine, similar to Canadian bacon

HOW YOU PRONOUNCE IT: pan cheh tuh

WHAT IT SAYS: **panini**

WHAT IT MEANS: a grilled sandwich of vegetables, cheese, and sometimes meat, served in focaccia (see *focaccia*)

HOW YOU PRONOUNCE IT: pah nee nee

WHAT IT SAYS: **Parmesan**

WHAT IT MEANS: a dry-textured, sharp-flavored Italian cheese, often grated

HOW YOU PRONOUNCE IT: pahr muh zahn

WHAT IT SAYS: **pâté**

WHAT IT MEANS: meat or fowl, finely minced or ground, seasoned and chilled in a loaf-shaped mold

HOW YOU PRONOUNCE IT: pah tay

WHAT IT SAYS: **penne**

WHAT IT MEANS: pasta cut on the diagonal into short tubes

HOW YOU PRONOUNCE IT: pen nay

WHAT IT SAYS: **pesto**

WHAT IT MEANS: an Italian sauce made of basil, garlic, pine nuts, olive oil, and grated cheese

HOW YOU PRONOUNCE IT: peh stoh

WHAT IT SAYS: **phyllo**

WHAT IT MEANS: tissue-thin sheets of pastry, used most often in Greek dishes

HOW YOU PRONOUNCE IT: fee loh

WHAT IT SAYS: **piccata**

WHAT IT MEANS: a style of serving thinly pounded cutlets of meat or chicken, sautéed in lemon and butter

HOW YOU PRONOUNCE IT: pih kah tuh

WHAT IT SAYS: **pilaf**

WHAT IT MEANS: a dish consisting of seasoned rice or grains mixed with onions, raisins, lentils or other legumes, dried fruits, or vegetables

HOW YOU PRONOUNCE IT: pee lahf

WHAT IT SAYS: **pistou**

WHAT IT MEANS: a sauce made of basil, garlic, and olive oil

HOW YOU PRONOUNCE IT: pees too

WHAT IT SAYS: **polenta**

WHAT IT MEANS: a thick mush made of cornmeal boiled in stock or water

HOW YOU PRONOUNCE IT: poh lehn tah

WHAT IT SAYS: **porcini**

WHAT IT MEANS: an edible mushroom with a thick stem and a plump, round top

HOW YOU PRONOUNCE IT: pohr chee nee

WHAT IT SAYS: **primavera**

WHAT IT MEANS: made with fresh vegetables; usually refers
to a cream sauce most often served with pasta

HOW YOU PRONOUNCE IT: pree muh vehr uh

WHAT IT SAYS: **prosciutto**

WHAT IT MEANS: a dry, spicy Italian ham, usually served
in paper-thin slices

HOW YOU PRONOUNCE IT: proh shoo toh

WHAT IT SAYS: **quesadilla**

WHAT IT MEANS: a wheat tortilla folded and filled with a
mixture of chicken or meat, vegetables, and cheese

HOW YOU PRONOUNCE IT: keh sah dee yah

WHAT IT SAYS: **quinoa**

WHAT IT MEANS: a weed, similar to wild rice, often served
in place of rice or other grains

HOW YOU PRONOUNCE IT: keen wah

WHAT IT SAYS: **radicchio**

WHAT IT MEANS: a red or purple member of the bitter-flavored chicory family of salad greens

HOW YOU PRONOUNCE IT: rah dee kee oh

WHAT IT SAYS: **ricotta**

WHAT IT MEANS: a soft Italian cheese, similar in texture to cottage cheese

HOW YOU PRONOUNCE IT: rih kaht tuh

WHAT IT SAYS: **rigatoni**

WHAT IT MEANS: a ribbed pasta, cut into short, slightly curved tubes

HOW YOU PRONOUNCE IT: rig ah toh nee

WHAT IT SAYS: **risotto**

WHAT IT MEANS: a rich, smooth dish of rice, cooked slowly with broth and sprinkled with cheese

HOW YOU PRONOUNCE IT: rih saw toh

WHAT IT SAYS: **roux**

WHAT IT MEANS: a mixture of butter and flour, cooked over low heat and used as a base for many sauces, particularly in Cajun cooking

HOW YOU PRONOUNCE IT: roo

WHAT IT SAYS: **saltimbocca**

WHAT IT MEANS: thinly pounded veal cutlets, stuffed with ham and cheese, seasoned with sage, and served with a wine sauce

HOW YOU PRONOUNCE IT: sahl tihm boh kuh

WHAT IT SAYS: **sashimi**

WHAT IT MEANS: very thinly sliced raw fish

HOW YOU PRONOUNCE IT: sah shee mee

WHAT IT SAYS: **scampi**

WHAT IT MEANS: large shrimp sautéed in olive oil and garlic

HOW YOU PRONOUNCE IT: scam pee

WHAT IT SAYS: **seviche**

WHAT IT MEANS: raw fish "cooked" in a marinade of lime or lemon juice

HOW YOU PRONOUNCE IT: seh vee chay

WHAT IT SAYS: **shallot**

WHAT IT MEANS: a small mild-flavored onion

HOW YOU PRONOUNCE IT: shal uht

WHAT IT SAYS: **sherbet**

WHAT IT MEANS: a frozen, icy dessert made with milk or cream, egg whites, and flavored with fruit juice

HOW YOU PRONOUNCE IT: sher biht

WHAT IT SAYS: **sorbet**

WHAT IT MEANS: a frozen, icy dish, served as a palate refresher or as a dessert, differing from sherbet in that it does not contain milk (see *sherbet*)

HOW YOU PRONOUNCE IT: sor bay

WHAT IT SAYS: **sorrel**

WHAT IT MEANS: leafy salad greens with a distinctive lemony flavor

HOW YOU PRONOUNCE IT: sor uhl

WHAT IT SAYS: **soufflé**

WHAT IT MEANS: a feather-light dish made of egg yolks and stiffly beaten egg whites, served either as a main dish or a dessert

HOW YOU PRONOUNCE IT: soo flay

WHAT IT SAYS: **squab**

WHAT IT MEANS: a young, farm-raised pigeon

HOW YOU PRONOUNCE IT: skwahb

WHAT IT SAYS: **Szechuan**

WHAT IT MEANS: a style of Chinese cooking noted for its use of hot peppers and spices

HOW YOU PRONOUNCE IT: sehch wahn

WHAT IT SAYS: **tagliatelle**

WHAT IT MEANS: pasta cut into narrow ribbons

HOW YOU PRONOUNCE IT: tah lyah teh leh

WHAT IT SAYS: **tapas**

WHAT IT MEANS: small snacks, originating in Spain, served as appetizers

HOW YOU PRONOUNCE IT: tah pas

WHAT IT SAYS: **tapenade**

WHAT IT MEANS: a purée of capers, black olives, anchovies, and olive oil, used as a spread for canapés and hors d'oeuvres

HOW YOU PRONOUNCE IT: ta puh nahd

WHAT IT SAYS: **tartare**

WHAT IT MEANS: raw steak, ground or cut into small strips, traditionally served with a raw egg as a garnish

HOW YOU PRONOUNCE IT: tar tar

WHAT IT SAYS: **terrine**

WHAT IT MEANS: a rough-textured pâté (see *pâté*)

HOW YOU PRONOUNCE IT: teh reen

WHAT IT SAYS: **timbale**

WHAT IT MEANS: a creamy mixture of meat or vegetables, cooked in a small cup-shaped mold

HOW YOU PRONOUNCE IT: tihm bah lay

WHAT IT SAYS: **tiramisù**

WHAT IT MEANS: an Italian dessert consisting of layers of sponge cake soaked with coffee or liquor, layered with mascarpone cheese, and topped with grated chocolate

HOW YOU PRONOUNCE IT: tih ruh mee soo

WHAT IT SAYS: **truffle**

WHAT IT MEANS: either a highly prized and pricey edible subterranean fungus or a rich, creamy chocolate

HOW YOU PRONOUNCE IT: truhf uhl

WHAT IT SAYS: **velouté**

WHAT IT MEANS: a smooth white sauce made with stock instead of milk

HOW YOU PRONOUNCE IT: veh loo tay

WHAT IT SAYS: **vinaigrette**

WHAT IT MEANS: a simple dressing of oil and vinegar, often flavored with mustard and garlic

HOW YOU PRONOUNCE IT: vihn uh greht

WHAT IT SAYS: **wasabi**

WHAT IT MEANS: a condiment, similar in flavor to horseradish, made from the root of an Asian plant

HOW YOU PRONOUNCE IT: wah sah bee

WHAT IT SAYS: **ziti**

WHAT IT MEANS: a medium-sized tubular pasta

HOW YOU PRONOUNCE IT: zee tee

Share and Share Alike

When dining in a restaurant, a gentleman and his dinner companion may wish to split an entrée between them, either for reasons of appetite or economy. In such cases, however, a gentleman is always wise to read the small print on the menu, because some restaurants add a surcharge if a dish is shared by two or more people. To avoid unpleasantness, he may simply ask the server, "We're thinking about sharing the beef Wellington. Do you think it will serve two people?" If the server and the establishment wish to preserve their integrity, the server will give an honest answer, saying, "Yes, couples share it quite often," or suggesting, "Yes, I think it probably could serve two, but you might like a salad or an appetizer to go along with it." If there is a charge for splitting beef Wellington between two diners, and if that policy is not noted on the menu, it is the server's responsibility to mention that fact at this point. It is highly unlikely that such a surcharge will actually double the cost of the entrée, but a gentleman should not be subjected to unpleasant surprises when he is presented with the bill.

5

THE JOB OF EATING

BUSINESS MEALS, ALL DAY LONG

Some of the most crucial moments in a
gentleman's professional life may well take place
over a meal. Whether he is being interviewed
for a job, attempting to close a sale, or asking a
wealthy acquaintance for a contribution to a
political campaign or a charitable cause, poor
table manners could very well mean the
difference between getting a great new job or
missing the chance of a lifetime, impressing a
new client or embarrassing his employer. A
gentleman knows that behaving himself at the
table is part of his job, a central part of the
work he does every day.

If a gentleman intends
to do business in a restaurant, he
always makes a reservation.

————

A gentleman shows up on time
for a business luncheon. He realizes
that being late is not only bad for
business—it is also rude behavior.

————

If his employer has
established a limit on a gentleman's
entertainment budget, he
sticks to it.

————

Even if a gentleman's
employer has given him the
go-ahead to splurge, a gentleman
does not abuse his boss's generosity.
He can "splurge" without ordering
the biggest steak on the menu
or the rarest bottle of wine
in the cellar.

————

When a gentleman is being entertained at a business luncheon or dinner, he waits for his host or hostess to take the lead before ordering the most expensive entrée or the most extravagant bottle of wine on the menu.

––––––

If a gentleman's company does not have a budget for elaborate entertaining, the gentleman chooses a restaurant where he is confident the prices will not send the company into bankruptcy.

––––––

When selecting a restaurant for a business luncheon or dinner, especially if he is not well acquainted with his clients and their taste in food, he makes his reservation at an establishment with a varied, mainstream menu.

––––––

If a gentleman intends to conduct
formal business during a meal—and
particularly if he requires flip charts
or PowerPoint presentations—he
requests a private dining room.

————

A gentleman knows
that it is his own behavior and his
own professionalism—not the
extravagance of the restaurant—that
will impress his clients and make
his company shine.

————

A gentleman does not
overindulge simply because he is a
guest, being entertained on another
person's expense account. A
gentleman never overindulges.

————

Doing Business

At a business breakfast, luncheon, or dinner, a gentleman's table manners remain as refined as if he were at a private dinner or a formal banquet. If he is invited to do business at the table, however, he makes it clear that he intends the occasion to be about the job at hand. He cuts through the chitchat in the most gentlemanly but straightforward way possible. It is not at all rude for him to pull a meandering conversation back on track with a simple, to-the-point question such as, "Now, Joanne, what about the Brinkley deal?"

Even if every one of his fellow diners decides to squander an opportunity to do business, a gentleman retains his dignity, his integrity, and his composure. He knows he need not play the good-old-boy game in order to get his work done. In the future, and if he has the option to do so, he may suggest that his clients or coworkers and he conduct their business over the conference table, perhaps with soda and sandwiches brought in for sustenance.

Extended dinner parties financed by corporate expense accounts, stoked by twenty-ounce steaks and fueled by liquor, are still a reality, but macho, cholesterol-chugging, three-martini luncheons are much less common than they used to be—especially since women have assumed more and more leadership roles in the corporate world.

If a business meal is held in the dining room of a restaurant, fine or not-so-fine, all the diners at the table turn off their cell phones. Or, at the very least, they turn their cell phones to the "vibrate" mode. As a gesture of consideration for diners at the nearby tables, as well as his own fellow diners, if a gentleman must talk on his cell phone, even about business matters, he leaves the table. The day is past when anybody was convinced of the urgent need for a diner to return, accept, or make a cell phone call in the middle of a restaurant.

At the end of a business breakfast, luncheon, or dinner, it is highly unlikely that a gentleman's clients will offer to help out with the bill. Once all the eating, drinking, coffee sipping, and deliberating are done, the host simply says to the server, "Give me the bill, please." It would be unusual, in the extreme, for him to encounter any protests or offers to share in the tip. If such offers should arise, though, he simply says, "No thanks. Parkley Sprockets is getting this."

INVITATIONS AT THE OFFICE

If a gentleman is invited to a dinner, or any other social occasion, by a coworker, he does not assume that everyone else in the office has been invited. Instead, unless the invitation has been posted on the break-room bulletin board, or has been distributed via an office-wide e-mail, he does not take it upon himself to ask a fellow employee, "Did you get invited to the Postons for Friday night?" or to say, "Guess I'll be seeing you at Mel and Larry's tomorrow. Right?"

A Gentleman on a Job Interview

On many occasions the job-interview experience may involve a meal—whether it is a breakfast, a luncheon, or a dinner. Such occasions allow a gentleman's potential employers to size up his personality and his social skills. They also allow the gentleman a glimpse into the corporate personality of the firm where he may be invited to work.

At job-interview meals, a few guidelines are worth remembering:

- A gentleman waits to follow the lead of his host, or others at the table, before he orders either food or drink.

- To prevent unsightliness in the midst of the interview process, a gentleman avoids ordering potentially sloppy dishes such as pasta—unless he is fully confident he can handle them without mishap.

- If the direction of the conversation seems to stray from the business at hand, the gentleman may attempt to redirect it by saying, "Multi-Net did awfully well last year, didn't it?"

- If his host suggests a restaurant where the gentleman cannot, may not, or wishes not to eat the food, he lets that fact be known as soon as possible. More often than not, however, he will not even be asked about his preferences before the location for a job-interview meal is established. In such cases, he does his best to find something on the menu he can eat.

- If the table conversation turns to topics that the gentleman finds unpleasant—or if jokes of a racist, ethnic, homophobic, or any other degrading nature crop up— he does not join in the conversation or pretend to find the jokes amusing. To preserve his own self-respect, he may choose to speak up, stating that he finds such comments offensive. Even if he chooses to remain silent, he will have learned an important lesson about the business where he may be asked to work. Such comments may, in fact, be a determining factor in his decision to accept or turn down the job offer.

- If a gentleman does not drink alcohol, he does not order alcohol, even if everybody else at the table is ordering it.

- On an interview, a gentleman is always well advised to monitor his alcohol intake. Even if his interviewers are in their cups, they will have second thoughts about an interviewee who must be folded into a taxi at the end of the evening.

6

STAND UP AND BE FED

COCKTAIL PARTIES AND BUFFET SUPPERS

Buffets and cocktail parties offer some of
life's most convivial experiences. On many
occasions no formal dining table is involved, and
guests are expected to stroll about, enjoying the
company of good friends or getting to know
new acquaintances. This does not mean,
however, that such events are not without their
almost unique challenges. They may demand
that a gentleman figure out how to juggle a
plate and a beverage, balancing both of them on
his lap. At such parties, in fact, a gentleman's
social skills may be put to the toughest test, but
these events may also offer him some of the best
times of his party-going life.

At a cocktail supper, or
any occasion where hors d'oeuvres
and canapés have been set out for the
guests, a gentleman does not sort
through the snacks in search of the
most luscious or largest morsel.
Neither does he pick out all the
cashews from the mixed nuts.

———

If a gentleman is hosting
a cocktail party, he invites only as
many people as can comfortably
enjoy themselves in his home.

———

If a gentleman is hosting a
cocktail party where he
provides alcohol, he must
also provide food.

———

When hosting any event
where alcohol is provided, a
gentleman always provides
nonalcoholic options.

———

A gentleman does not attend a party to which he has not been specifically invited—unless he is assured that the host has insisted that all his friends "bring anybody" they know.

———

At a buffet dinner, once a gentleman has filled his plate to an appropriate level, he need not wait for all the other guests to wend their way through the line before he begins eating. In such situations, however, he waits until at least a couple of other guests have filled their plates and joined him. He does not dine alone.

———

Even if he is not well acquainted with anyone else in the room, once he has filled his plate, a gentleman seats himself near another guest, or a group of guests, and attempts to begin a conversation, either by introducing himself or by saying, "My, isn't this pork roast beautiful?"

———

A gentleman does not station himself by the food table at a cocktail party, feeding himself off the serving platters.

———

A gentleman never places his glass or his coffee cup directly on a piece of furniture, even if that piece of furniture is a glass-top coffee table. He knows that a sweaty glass will leave damp rings even on glass or stone, while the heat from hot coffee will leave circles of steam on any surface.

———

If a gentleman is offered a coaster or a cocktail napkin, he uses it.

———

If a gentleman is not offered a coaster or a cocktail napkin, he asks for one.

———

STANDING INVITATIONS

While a sit-down dinner party for eight or ten people can be one of life's loveliest experiences, a gentleman may find that such occasions are increasingly rare today. Instead, more often than not, he will find himself invited to a sizable "cocktail supper" with a substantial spread of hors d'oeuvres and canapés, or he will discover that the evening's repast has been spread out on a sideboard or on the dining room table. Earlier in the day, if a gentleman is invited for brunch, he will probably be right to assume that a buffet of rich egg-based casseroles, breads, bacon, sausage, and fruit awaits him. In such situations, he is expected to serve himself and find his own place to settle in the living room, den, or even on a convenient staircase.

Such occasions allow the host or hostess to entertain a goodly number of friends on a single occasion. Thus, a lavish buffet may turn out to be a considerably grander experience than a sit-down dinner, with much milling about and lively chatter. In such situations, although the spirit of the evening may be somewhat casual, a gentleman does not assume, simply because he must fill his own plate, that he may let his good manners lapse.

At any cocktail supper or buffet dinner, a gentleman must greet his host or hostess immediately upon his arrival. Within seconds, if the party is being run correctly, he will be offered a drink, by his host or hostess or by a server. If a full bar is available, he may be asked, "May I get you something to drink?" If the offerings are less varied, he will be asked, "Would you like a glass of wine?" or "May I get you a beer?" If a gentleman does not drink alcohol, he simply says, "I'd love a soda or a glass of water, if that's available."

During the cocktail hour, a gentleman's goal is to make pleasant conversation with his fellow guests. (He does not attempt to monopolize his host or hostess.) He may strike up a chat with any other guest, particularly if he and the other guest find themselves standing in line at the bar or side by side in the buffet line. No matter how enjoyable that conversation, however, a gentleman and his fellow guest do not linger at the bar or at the serving table so long as to impede the flow of traffic. They take their drinks or fill their plates, and then move out into the larger world of the party.

At a cocktail supper, or even the simplest cocktail party, a gentleman may find a great variety of bite-sized foods. If a stack of small plates is offered, he takes one and proceeds to make his selection from the table. Especially if he is consuming alcohol, a gentleman is well advised to enjoy a substantial selection of the treats that are offered to him. He does not, however, load his plate to overflowing, giving the impression that he has not eaten all day—or that he is intent on taking undue advantage of his host or hostess's hospitality. The same applies to his consumption of alcohol, if it is offered.

At a buffet supper or at a brunch, a gentleman will find plates, knives, forks, and napkins arranged on the buffet table, ready for his use. In some cases the plates will be at one end of the buffet table, with the flatware (wrapped in napkins) at the other end. In other cases, both the plates and the flatware will be set out at the start of the buffet line, thus requiring the gentleman to perform a nimble juggling act as he proceeds through the line. As he approaches the buffet line, a gentleman keeps his wits about him, taking his place in line and following in the direction in which the other guests seem to be moving. He understands that all his food, including the salad, entrée, and side dishes, are expected to go on his one dinner plate. Separate plates will be offered for dessert, but only later in the evening. Even if the dessert is already set out on a sideboard, a gentleman understands that he will have the opportunity to return later in the evening to enjoy that treat.

At a large party, a gentleman may discover that

duplicate dishes have been set out on both sides of
the table. If such is the case, he takes his servings
from one side of the table. He does not find it
necessary to check out the other side of the table,
in hopes of finding better cuts of tenderloin or
more luscious slices of the chocolate truffle cake.

At the best of all possible buffets, at the end of
the serving line a gentleman will be offered a lap
tray, sizable enough to hold his plate, his
flatware, and his glass. Once he has found a place
where he can comfortably sit, he settles himself in
and balances his tray on his lap. If he finds that
his glass seems to sit unsteadily on his tray, he
places his glass on some convenient flat surface,
provided that surface is unlikely to be damaged
by the bottom of a damp glass. When all else
fails, a gentleman places his glass on the floor
beside him, keeping it within ready reach and
watching out for unintentionally clumsy guests.

If lap trays are not offered, a gentleman simply
spreads his napkin on his lap and balances his
plate on top of it. He takes special care not to saw

away at his food with his knife and fork, lest he send a chunk of pork roast sailing across the room.

A gentleman may return to the buffet for a second helping, if he desires one. He does not allow himself to be seen scraping the bottom of the casserole dish, however. If fresh plates are still available on the table or the sideboard, he may take one, or he may serve himself on the dinner plate he is already using, just as if he were in his own home. When serving himself from a buffet in a public restaurant, however, he remembers that health department guidelines most likely will require that he take a fresh plate each time he returns to the buffet table.

When it is time for dessert, the host or hostess, or a server, probably will come through the room, picking up dinner plates and used flatware. If his fellow diners all seem to have finished eating, a gentleman surrenders his plate as well. He does not say, "Wait a minute, I'm still eating my chicken." Dessert may then be served to him on an individual plate, or his host or hostess may say, "There's fresh peach cobbler in the dining room. I hope you'll try it."

Once all the trays have been picked up and the plates have been cleared away, a gentleman may linger among his fellow guests for as long as he pleases, provided it does not appear that he will be the last guest to be shooed out the door. Whenever he makes his departure, a gentleman makes sure to bid farewell directly to his host or hostess, thanking them for their hospitality and for their kindness in including him in a lovely occasion. If the party has been hosted by a number of people, the gentleman need only say "thank you" and "good night" to one or two of his hosts or hostesses. He makes a particular effort to express his thanks to the owners of the house where the party is taking place. When a party has been hosted by a number of people, he sends his thank-you note to the host or hostess who graciously welcomed a houseful of guests into his or her home.

How to Set Up a Buffet

When a gentleman serves a buffet-style meal in his own home, he carefully arranges the table so that his guests can comfortably serve themselves. He includes everything they will need to enjoy their meal and provides easy access to the food (preferably positioning the table in the middle of the room).

Whether the buffet is a table set against the wall, a table in the middle of the room, or the

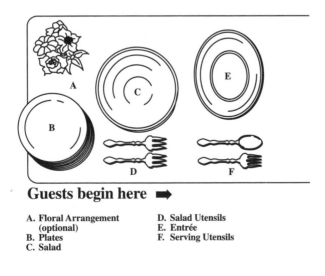

Guests begin here ➡

A. Floral Arrangement
   (optional)
B. Plates
C. Salad

D. Salad Utensils
E. Entrée
F. Serving Utensils

kitchen counter, guests will move alongside it in a single line. Accordingly, a gentleman stacks the plates at the beginning of the line and places the flatware, rolled in napkins, at the end of the line, which gives guests a free hand to serve themselves.

The gentleman places a serving spoon or fork with every dish on the buffet. He may serve beverages from a separate table. Flowers are a nice touch, provided they do not take up too much room.

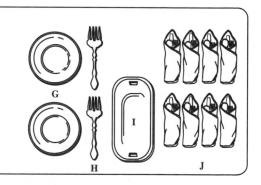

G. Side Dishes
H. Serving Utensils
I. Bread Platter
J. Flatware/Napkins

Gathering the Group

A good host attempts to give his guests plenty of notice. Two weeks lead time is appropriate for a dinner party. One week is sufficient for a more casual gathering.

Whether he offers his invitation in writing or by phone, he makes sure to answer all the questions his guests might logically have. For written invitations, a gentleman makes sure to include the nature of the party (cocktails, supper, brunch, a birthday party for Sue Ellen, or whatever), the date, the hour, the address, specifics about what to wear, and the information his guests need in order to reply. If his guests will need instructions about parking, he includes those as well.

If a host needs an accurate head count, he requests a reply by writing either "RSVP" or, more directly, "Please reply" at the bottom of his invitation, making sure to include his phone number. If his prospective guests have not responded by a reasonable time (forty-eight hours before the party), he may gracefully ask whether or not they plan to attend.

7

THE GHASTLY TABLE

DEALING WITH DINING DISASTERS

At any time, in a restaurant or at a private dinner party, a gentleman may discover that something unattractive or inedible is stuck between his teeth, or he has put some inedible morsel in his mouth. At such moments he need not feel debilitating embarrassment. The solution is, in fact, quite simple. If the objectionable morsel may be removed with his fork or spoon, that's the utensil he uses. If he can use his fingers to clean an errant string of spinach from his lips, he does so, using his napkin to mask his action and then disposing of the unsightly item on his plate. He feels no need to mention his difficulty to his dinner companions. Such unpleasantness, after all, is likely to be part of any gentleman's life.

Other problems may arise, however.

IF A GENTLEMAN DISCOVERS HE HAS SPILLED
SOUP OR GRAVY OR ANY OTHER SAUCE ON HIS
SHIRTFRONT, HIS PANTS FRONT, OR HIS TIE . . .

Even if he is dining among his closest friends or family members, and even if they are dining in a private home, a gentleman excuses himself from the table, offering no explanation—not even a self-effacing one such as, "Well, look what a mess I've made of myself." In the bathroom, he assesses the damage. If he has soiled his shirt or his trousers, he uses a napkin, dampened with a bit of *cold* water to attempt to remove or at least lessen the stain. Even if he cannot remove the stain at that very moment, he will at least make it easier for the dry cleaner or the washing machine to remove it the next day.

If a gentleman discovers a dribble of soup or sauce on his tie, however, he must be much more careful. In almost every case, after excusing himself from the table and reaching the bathroom, he blots the stain lightly with a napkin or a bit of tissue. If he is particularly savvy and is fully confident that he knows whether the stain is oil based or wine or water based, he may attempt to rub the stain briskly—using a tiny bit of warm water if the stain is oil based, or cold water if no grease is involved. In either case, however, a gentleman takes a great risk of spoiling a good silk tie.

If he finds himself in a men's room where an attendant is on hand, he may simply say, "Looks as if I've done some damage here. What do you think I should do?" The attendant may, in fact, be knowledgeable about removing stains and may have fabric-cleaning supplies on hand. If he does not solve the gentleman's problem—or even if he makes the problem worse—the gentleman does not complain. He has, after all, asked for the assistance, with no guarantee that it will work. In any case, if the attendant has attempted to fix the problem, the gentleman offers a grateful gratuity before returning to the party.

Should a gentleman notice that another diner has dropped a bit of soup or sauce on his shirt, pants, or tie, the gentleman simply advises him, ever so quietly, "Gerry, I believe you've got a bit of Hollandaise sauce there on your shirt." It is precisely the same courtesy a gentleman offers to a friend whose fly has been left unzipped.

IF A GENTLEMAN DISCOVERS A PROBLEM WITH THE BILL IN A RESTAURANT . . .

Although a gentleman does not pull out a calculator, or a pad and pencil, he is not ashamed to review the bill in a restaurant before he pays it. If he discovers that he has been overcharged, or undercharged, he calls the server discreetly to his side and points out the error. If there have been problems with the service earlier in the evening— for example, if an entrée has been unacceptable and the server has assured the guest that there will be no charge for it or that a complimentary dessert will be provided—and that correction is not noted on the bill, a gentleman points out that error as well. If the server immediately goes about correcting the error, the gentleman simply assumes the error is a human foible. If the server attempts to argue with the gentleman, the gentleman asks to see a manager.

IF A GENTLEMAN'S CREDIT CARD IS DECLINED IN A RESTAURANT . . .

In such situations a gentleman does not call attention to an already awkward state of affairs. He does not leap to the defensive, proclaiming, "Well, I'm sure there's a huge credit limit on that card," "I paid that bill over a month ago," or "Somebody's computer must be screwed up." Instead, he leaves the table along with the server, asking, "Would you mind running the card through again?" Even if the gentleman is confident that his credit is good, if the card continues to be declined, and if he does not have enough ready cash to cover the bill and the tip, he asks if he may pay by check, visit the nearest ATM, or return the next day with cash. If the establishment declines any and all of these gentlemanly offers—and if he is not offered the

option of washing dishes to work off the debt—
the gentleman has no recourse except to return
to the table and throw himself upon the mercy of
his friends, who will probably agree to chip in, if
their own finances permit. A gentleman repays
their kindness within the next twenty-four hours,
repaying them in cash. A gentleman does not let
such debts linger.

IF A GENTLEMAN DROPS FOOD ON THE
TABLECLOTH OR ON THE FLOOR . . .

A gentleman does not call attention to the
situation by exclaiming, "Oops!" or "Clumsy me!"
If he has dropped a sizeable chunk of food or a
considerable amount of sauce, his only recourse
is to use his napkin to retrieve the dropped food
or to blot up the sauce. He hopes that his host or
hostess will be alert enough to say, "Thank you,
Alan, for taking care of that. Let me get you a
fresh napkin." If such is not the case, he alerts his
host or hostess, or a server, saying, "Excuse me,
but I believe I could use a fresh napkin." When

the fresh napkin is provided, a gentleman makes no further explanation, exchanging it, without comment, for the soiled linen.

IF A GENTLEMAN BELCHES, AUDIBLY, AT THE DINNER TABLE . . .

A gentleman realizes that the frailties of the flesh may creep up on any one of us, at any time. A gentleman may use his napkin to stifle a discreet burp, but if a loud frog-croaking belch overcomes him, he must simply say, "Excuse me, please." A gentleman may only be forgiven for such unpleasantness once during a meal, however. If he discovers that he has been overcome by indigestion, he must head for the bathroom, in search of a sip of water. His next option is to ask his host or hostess for a glass of soda water. (Asking for an antacid tablet probably will not solve the problem immediately.) His final recourse is simply to inform his host or hostess, and his spouse or date, that he must depart, offering his regrets as sincerely and as expeditiously as possible.

IF A GENTLEMAN KNOCKS OVER A GLASS OF
WATER, WINE, OR ICED TEA, OR A CUP OF COFFEE . . .

If no breakage has occurred, a gentleman's first
instinct is to grab his napkin and attempt to sop
up the mess. His dinner companions may offer
their napkins as well, and a gentleman gladly
accepts that assistance. If he is in a private home,
his host or hostess will probably rise to help clean
up. If he is in a well-attended restaurant, a server
will materialize, almost out of nowhere, to provide
assistance. If the spillage involves red wine, strong
iced tea, or coffee, his host or hostess may attempt
a quick application of cold water to the stain.

In any case, though, a gentleman can do
nothing except say, "Excuse me for making such a
mess." He assumes that his host or hostess, or the
server, will provide him and his fellow guests with
fresh napkins. A thoughtful host or hostess—or a
responsible server—will provide a clean napkin to
cover the damp stain on the table.

On the way out the door, or when he writes
his thank-you note, the gentleman may remember

to say, "I hope you'll forgive my clumsiness with the wine glass." Otherwise, he says nothing more. Such accidents are an almost inevitable part of entertaining, or being entertained.

IF A GENTLEMAN FINDS THE FOOD IN A
RESTAURANT INEDIBLE OR THE DRINKS
UNDRINKABLE . . .

It makes no difference whether he is paying for his own dinner or whether he is another person's guest. There is no reason why a gentleman must soldier on, gnawing his way through a semi-raw steak or a stringy breast of chicken. He makes no apology for telling the server, "I'd like my steak cooked medium, not medium rare, please," or "My chicken is overcooked—would you ask the chef to try again, please?" If it appears that the gentleman's steak, once it returns, has simply been reheated under the microwave, the gentleman remains firm, saying, "I'd like a fresh steak. Please do not reheat this one." If the problem continues, he asks to speak to a manager.

The same advice applies if a gentleman finds his cocktail too weak, his coffee overbrewed, or his tea too strong. As a patron of the restaurant, he has a right to ask for his food to be served the way he wants it. If he learns, however, that a particular establishment's food is not cooked or served the way he prefers, he avoids that establishment in the future, thus saving himself, and the establishment, any further anguish.

IF A GENTLEMAN'S CHILDREN ARE MISBEHAVING, EITHER AT A RESTAURANT OR AT A DINNER IN A PRIVATE HOME . . .

It is every parent's prerogative to discipline children in the way he or she sees fit. In public places or at a dinner party, brunch, luncheon, or luau, however, a gentleman recognizes that his children's misbehavior may very likely disrupt the meal for his dinner companions or the other diners in the restaurant—even if it is a fast-food establishment. In such cases, a gentleman does not attempt to discipline his child in public, thus risking the possibility that fellow diners will be asked to share in even more unpleasantness. Instead, he takes the child away from the table, exercising appropriate discipline in a restroom, in the corner of a parking lot, or in the family automobile. If the child will not amend his or her behavior, or bursts into loud wails, a gentleman asks his server to provide to-go boxes for the food of all his family members. Once the food has been packed up, the gentleman, his child, and the rest of the family depart as swiftly and as discreetly as possible.

IF AN ARGUMENT OCCURS AT THE DINNER TABLE . . .

A gentleman enjoys friends who have strong opinions, but he also knows that out-and-out arguing does not aid digestion. If he discovers that the conversation is threatening to grow contentious, he simply says, "Now, friends, let's change the subject." If he is the host at a sizable dinner party, he may have to rise from his seat and play referee. If his guests refuse to behave themselves, he may even ask that they change seats, simply to get away from each other.

If the argument seems to have been fueled by alcohol, the gentleman suggests that they abstain from any further drinking. In the worst possible circumstances, when the enjoyment of his other guests or other people in a restaurant is threatened, a gentleman may be forced to say, "Tom and Tammy, I'm afraid this is getting out of hand. I must ask you either to end this conversation, or take it to the sidewalk." If the problem continues, without choosing sides, the gentleman must ask both of his argumentative friends to leave.

IF A GENTLEMAN DROPS A STEAK ON THE KITCHEN FLOOR OR ON THE DECK BESIDE THE GRILL . . .

Nobody need know what happens in the privacy of a gentleman's own kitchen. If he is cooking in the presence of his guests, however, he must express at least *some* concern over a steak that has slipped off the spatula and onto the gravel. If a replacement steak is available, he says, "I'm afraid this one is headed to the garbage." If no replacement is available, he suggests that he and another guest (preferably his date or a very close friend) share one of the larger steaks. He may be perfectly willing to take the gravel-encrusted steak to the kitchen, rinse it off, and grill it for himself. Unfortunately, some of his guests may find even that solution absolutely unpalatable.

IF A GENTLEMAN DISCOVERS THAT THE UTENSILS SET BEFORE HIM ARE DIRTY . . .

If a gentleman is dining in a restaurant, he simply asks his server for replacements, saying, "I don't think this spoon is quite clean. May I have another?" In such circumstances, when a gentleman is a guest in a private home, he faces an additional challenge. Still, he attempts to call as little attention as possible to the awkward moment.

After taking his place at the table, he does not

immediately inspect the flatware and then declare, "Otto, it looks like you need to run this spoon through the dishwasher again." Instead, once his food has been put before him, he simply asks his host, "Otto, could I have a fresh salad fork?" The gentleman hopes that, when Otto comes to replace the salad fork, he will check to make sure the other flatware is in better shape.

If a gentleman wishes to play games, he may choose to drop the soiled utensil on the floor, thus creating an excuse for requesting a replacement. Unfortunately, if the dinner knife and the dessert fork are soiled as well, he may end up requiring his host or hostess to run a relay race between the dinner table and the silver chest.

IF A GENTLEMAN IS PRESENTED WITH FOOD HE CANNOT EAT . . .

A gentleman attempts to prevent this sort of awkwardness, for himself and for his host or hostess, by paying attention to what might be served to him. If he has food allergies, when he is invited for dinner, he makes it a point to inform his host or hostess, saying, "It's probably best to tell you I have a food allergy. I'm allergic to nuts [or shellfish or flour]. But otherwise I can eat anything." A gentleman trusts that his host or hostess will be grateful for his frankness.

When he sits down at the table, nevertheless, a gentleman may still be served a course he cannot eat. He may leave the food untouched, or he may simply decline to take any of it when it is offered to him. He may choose to eat a bit of bread and butter, but if his host or hostess asks him, "Frank, is there something wrong?" he replies truthfully by simply saying, "This looks lovely, but I can't eat shellfish." His host or hostess then attempts to provide an alternative course.

If a gentleman's religion restricts him from eating any dish, however, he makes no pretense. If his host or hostess asks him why he is not eating the shrimp cocktail, he says, "Thanks, but

I don't eat shellfish." He does not say, "Sorry, but I don't eat shellfish." A gentleman does not apologize for his beliefs.

On the other hand, if a gentleman simply does not care for the food placed before him, he finds something else on the plate that he can eat, or he takes a couple of bites of the lamb chop, even if he hates lamb.

IF A GENTLEMAN BECOMES ILL AT THE TABLE . . .

Perhaps it's because of the salmon (that wasn't sufficiently smoked) or the hot asparagus soup (that wasn't quite hot enough) or the pork roast (that wasn't roasted to 160 degrees). Or maybe it's the leftover tuna sandwich that he had for lunch earlier in the day. For whatever reason, if a gentleman finds himself ill, either at a private dinner or in a restaurant, he must leave the table immediately, heading for a bathroom. If he feels no better after visiting the bathroom, he informs his host or hostess that he must leave, and his spouse or date must depart with him.

Meanwhile, in the most horrific of all circumstances, a gentleman may be overtaken by sudden nausea, actually become sick to his stomach, and even throw up at the table. Such moments steal up on even the best-mannered gentleman. He may inevitably feel embarrassed by the moment, but unless his illness has been brought on by overindulgence, he feels no personal guilt. He is remorseful and assists his host or hostess in straightening up the table, if he feels well enough to do so. In most cases, however, he will be better advised to retreat to the bathroom, wipe his face with a cool towel, and depart as quickly as possible.

In writing his thank-you note for the evening, a gentleman does not avoid the reality of what has taken place. Instead, he states frankly, "Your dinner party was lovely. I hope my illness did not ruin the evening for you and your other guests." In such instances, a gentleman may wish to accompany his thank-you note with a small bouquet of flowers. If his illness persists, however, his host or hostess may wish to send *him* a get-well note.

IF A GENTLEMAN SUSPECTS, IN THE AFTERMATH OF A DINNER PARTY, THAT HE HAS FOOD POISONING . . .

If a gentleman finds himself ill after a private dinner party, cooked by the hosts themselves, he can do little except let bygones be bygones. (If such illness becomes a regular occurrence after dinner in a particular home, however, a gentleman may rethink accepting invitations to that house.) He may mention his illness to the other guests, to ascertain whether it is his stomach that is at fault, or the food. But nothing is accomplished by calling his host or hostess and saying, "Last night was great, but I ended up spending six hours in the emergency room."

If the food has been provided by a caterer, however, the gentleman does let his hosts know that there has been a problem. The same advice applies if he has dined in a restaurant and has become ill afterward. Professional caterers and restaurants are expected to abide by strict health department regulations if they are to keep their licenses. The gentleman may elect not to patronize a restaurant, should he be suspicious of its cleanliness. But his host or hostess *must* be informed if it appears that a caterer's food has made him ill, so that they may refrain from using that catering company again.

IF A GENTLEMAN EVEN SUSPECTS THAT ONE OF HIS DINNER COMPANIONS IS CHOKING AND IS IN NEED OF ASSISTANCE . . .

If a dinner companion begins choking on his food, and continues to do so, even for a split second, a gentleman springs into action. If the gentleman knows how to apply the Heimlich maneuver, he does so. If he is not trained in the Heimlich maneuver, however, he does not risk causing further damage by applying his personal version of the maneuver. If he is in a restaurant, where servers are usually trained to help in such situations, he calls for assistance, loudly and firmly. If he is at a private dinner party, and if no other guest rises to the occasion, he calls out, "Does anybody here know the Heimlich?" (In this instance, a gentleman is allowed to shout if needed.) If there is no response, and unless he knows some certain other means of loosening an obstruction from the windpipe, he calls 911 and asks for immediate assistance. He does not assume that he can drive the choking victim to the emergency room in his own car.

A gentleman is best advised to consult his local chapter of the American Red Cross for thorough training in the Heimlich maneuver. He does not assume that he knows how to save a life simply because he has seen a step-by-step chart in a restroom.